NEW YORK'S

50 BEST

NEW YORK'S 50 BEST

Museums for **COOL** Parents and Their **KIDS**

Alfred Gingold
and Helen Rogan

Illustrations by
Catherine Lazure

A CITY & COMPANY GUIDE * NEW YORK

Library of Congress Cataloging-in-Publication Data
is available upon request.
ISBN 1-885492-83-9
First Edition
Printed in the United States of America

To dear Toby,
who agreed to come along—mostly.

ACKNOWLEDGEMENTS

We would like to thank the following people for helping us in
the preparation of our book: Anna French of the Weeksville
Society, Ken Moss of the Dyckman Farmhouse Museum,
Vivienne Shaffer of Lefferts Homestead, Juanita Lanzó of the
Bronx Museum of the Arts, Peter Stolz and Sir John Wemyss-
Kessler of the National Parks Service. Any factual errors we've
made are our responsibility alone. Thanks also to Judith
Sonntag for her sensitive copy-editing. As always, we're
grateful to Helene Silver and Heather Drucker of City &
Company, and especially to Melisa Coburn, our smart and
gracious editor.

PUBLISHER'S NOTE

10 9 8 7 6 5 4 3 2 1

Contents

Introduction

It is widely accepted that museums and children don't mix, except during school trips, even among New Yorkers, for whom cultural treasures are an everyday fact of life. Mention a family museum trip to most parents, and they'll roll their eyes or make jokes about dragging the kids along in handcuffs. We feel their pain. But, as the seasoned authors of *The Cool Parents Guide to All of New York,* we beg to differ. We *know* that  museum trips can be fun for everyone, if you, the parents, are prepared to be smart and flexible. And, with this book, we offer help—for eager, optimistic tourists as well as weary locals who need an infusion of energy.

New York City contains a vast and incredibly diverse array of museums, from immense institutions to little gems. The greatest concentration is in Manhattan, but there are museums worth visiting in all five boroughs. They celebrate just about every area of human achievement. The NYPD has its own museum, and so does the NYFD.

New York has museums in forts, farmhouses, and townhouses, on a barge, on an aircraft carrier, and in a subway station. In one day, you can see a classic helicopter (at MoMA), Al Capone's tommy gun (at the Police Museum), George Washington's Bible and Abraham Lincoln's hat (at Federal Hall and the Forbes Magazine Gallery, respectively). Still not satisfied? Try looking at ethnic folk art, Victorian dollhouses, antique moccasins, van Goghs, moon rocks, and, in a Tibetan museum on Staten Island, more mysterious, gleaming statues of Buddha than you've ever seen in one place. Incidentally, when did you last go to the Statue of Liberty?

Common sense tells us that it should be possible for you all to have an enjoyable time at these spectacular sites. All it takes is a little planning and that special ability all truly cool parents develop, sooner or later, out of sheer self-protectiveness—knowing when enough is enough. We've made it easy for you, by selecting a mix of the tried and true, the unfamiliar and the slightly weird. Some of our biggest and best museums are so renowned that they can seem intimidating. We suggest unintimidating ways to approach them. We've also explored lesser-known, farther-flung places that can be just as rewarding as the biggies. With a little preparation and the right attitude, you and yours will have fun—stimulating, edifying fun, maybe, but still fun. We guarantee it.

But only if you call first. Few things can ruin a family trip faster than finding your destination closed or the exhibition you wanted to see gone. Hours of operation change, admission charges change, exhibitions move. We've provided phone numbers; make that call! (And while you've got them on the phone, ask about additional programs and special events for kids. Many of the institutions in this book have them.) A museum's website can also be an excellent source of information. We've included addresses for the museums that have sites, and a good number are worth checking out.

Subways are faster and easier for kids to handle than buses, so we've provided subway directions whenever possible. You can get bus directions at 718-330-1234, a Transit Authority help line that's actually helpful.

We've suggested age ranges for kids visiting the museums. Take our suggestions with a grain of salt. You know what's appropriate for your child better than anyone else does.

Museums Without Pain

10

Tips for Visiting

1 Just Do It

Make your own plan before going. Don't consult with the kids or provide choices. This can only muddy the water. When you're there, stride firmly toward your choices. Don't mill about. Of course, if they clamor to look at something that seems promising, take them right over.

2 Be Prepared

Just as you've prepared, prime them if necessary. Make sure they know something about immigrants arriving in New York if you're going to the Tenement Museum; or get some juicy facts about Theodore Roosevelt if you're going to his birthplace. (Did you know he carried 18 spare pairs of spectacles when he charged up San Juan Hill?) They'll feel better about going, and they'll get more out of it while they're there.

3 Be Brief

Focus on the things you've picked or the things that tickle them, and then get out of there. If you stay only 45 minutes or an hour, you'll still have accomplished something, and they'll be more willing to come along next time.

4 Tourist Class

For some museums, such as military installations or historic homes, it's really helpful to take an organized tour. A portrait that looks like just another gloomy face to you might turn out to have an interesting or creepy story behind it or a noteworthy squirrel in the background. But if the tour guide isn't keeping your kids' attention, have the courage to walk away!

5 Art, Schmart

Kids aren't scared of art—most of them love it—and will approach whatever you put in front of them with a fresh, questioning gaze. One caveat, though: The Old Masters, with their classical themes, murky backgrounds and big-boned naked ladies, tend to turn kids off. So, wait a few years for Rembrandt and Rubens.

6 Gimmicks Work

Always have a few up your sleeve. In a room full of artifacts or paintings, split up and each take a side. Then meet up, report which was the best thing and why, and switch sides. (Make sure you're listening as much as talking.) Or play another game, such as I Spy.

7 Your Gifted Child

If your child begins to pout and fret before you've even gone inside, head immediately for the gift shop and collaborate in picking out the nicest postcards there. Then make it your mission to go looking for the originals.

8 Feed the Body, Then the Soul

To head off pouting and fretting, make sure that everyone has eaten before embarking.

9 Phone First

See whether there are any special programs or events that day. Also check to see whether the museum has a treasure hunt/discovery sheet/special activity booklet for kids. The thrill of the chase makes everything more interesting. (Armed with a quiz, our son once got briefly interested in a lot of rusty old farm implements in an English village museum.)

10 Bribe 'Em

(See Great Museum Gift Shops, page 148) Set a price limit, and let them choose. With any luck, someday they'll grow out of that terrible need to buy something, *anything*.

Alice Austen House Museum

2 Hylan Boulevard at Edgewater St.
Staten Island   718-816-4506
www.preserve.org/hht/hht.htm
Closed: Mon., Tues., Wed.,
all of Jan. and Feb.

All ages

Getting there: 1, 9, N, or R to South Ferry, then S51 bus to Bay Street/ Hylan Boulevard. Or take the Bay Street exit off the Verrazano-Narrows Bridge, and turn off at Hylan Boulevard.

Right on the Staten Island shore, facing Brooklyn and across the street from a hideous high-rise, sits the charming, diminutive Alice Austen House. It started life in 1690 as a one-room Dutch farmhouse and was later transformed by Alice's grandparents into a Victorian gingerbread fantasy that they named Clear Comfort. Alice grew up at Clear Comfort, inherited the house, and lived there comfortably for 80 years. For much of that time she took extraordinary photographs—of clipper ships and ocean liners coming into the harbor, of the society tennis parties and picnics favored by her moneyed set ("the larky life," she called it), of immigrants in

quarantine or newsboys on the Lower East Side. This house is her memorial and an exhibition space for some of her work (thousands of her glass negatives are still stored at the Staten Island Historical Society).

This tranquil place will interest children for several reasons. First, the little house itself, which, with its Dutch doors, low ceilings, wide-board floors, and elaborate Victorian furniture, has the feel of a dollhouse. Then, covering many of the downstairs walls are the photographs of Alice's vanished world, which will have an immediate appeal for you and also for the kids if you explain her story: She developed an interest in photography at the age of 10. Untutored, she became accomplished but never did anything with her work. Her family lost everything in the Depression, and eventually, at the age of 80, Alice became homeless. An enterprising magazine editor who had come across her work went looking for her and found her in the local poorhouse. He spoke to her but she didn't respond—until he held up a couple of her negatives. Her face lit up, and she told him about the pictures. The editor swiftly sold enough of her work that she could be moved to a private nursing-home to live out her days. (All this information and more is contained in a video that you can see in the right-hand parlor. Unfortunately, it's an hour long and will tax the patience of your children.)

Above all, there's the location. Fourteen acres of gently rolling lawn slope right down to a rocky beach, littered with enticing debris—driftwood, beach glass, tires, mysterious tubing, and no medical waste that we could spot. Right in front of you is the entrance to New York Harbor, with its spectacular sea traffic. To your right is the majestic sweep of the Verrazano-Narrows Bridge, to your left the Manhattan skyline. It's especially stirring to be out there when there's a nautical festival going on, with appropriate music and knot tying. (Call for details about special events.) And the view is all the more remarkable when you consider that you're standing in the garden of a little white house with filigree decoration and a long Dutch roof.

American Museum of Natural History

Central Park West at 79th Street
212-769-5100 *www.amnh.org*
Closed: Thanksgiving and Christmas Day

All ages

**Getting there:
B or C to
81st Street;
1 or 9 to
79th Street**

There's something greatly reassuring about a trip to the American Museum of Natural History. Your children probably know it better than you do—unless you're a former New York City kid yourself, in which case you, too, will have made innumerable class trips through its dim halls to peer at Native American longhouses, naked Neanderthals (big thrill!), and the totem poles of the Kwakiutl. Novices or habitues, you'll all sink gratefully into its cool, enveloping aura. Even when it's crammed with scuttling kids and roving bands of tourists, it retains a serenity you can find only at world-class institutions with the confidence to survive any old fad of the day. Interactivity, for example. (Still not a big deal here.)

The most modern part of the museum is the new Hall of Biodiversity, a truly staggering room, with its rainforest (featuring such stalwarts of nature documentaries as the hydrax, the potto, and the pangolin) and its great chain of being—from bacteria and lichen to amphibians, mammals and crustaceans. Fifteen hundred or so forms of life are exquisitely modeled and placed, some on the wall, some in the air. The endangered animals in their huge glass case seem particularly noble. On video screens (this is the modern part) you can watch film strips about all the world's ecosystems (wetlands, deserts, and such) and threats to them (deforestation, alteration of habitat, and the like). A few minutes' exposure to all this may actually give your child a sense of nature's complex web of connections.

The other big favorite is, of course, the dinosaur exhibit on the fourth floor—two halls of enormous skeletons in very peppy poses, tails waving, jaws wide and ready for action. If you're looking for the true giants, go to the Saurischian hall; don't miss the Tyrannosaurus rex skull and the Apatosaurus (which you actually cannot miss, since it towers above everything and has an oddly tiny skull). Triceratops, Stegosaurus, and assorted duck-billed friends are in the Ornithischian hall. Here, again, the kids will feel totally at home, as a result of the enduring fascination the world's smallest people have for the world's largest creatures.

For us, the indisputable stars of the show remain the dioramas, particularly the North American mammals on the first floor and the African mammals on the second and third, with the majestic group of elephants residing on the second floor. The animals in their cases are forever frozen on guard, in combat or play, against delicately painted backdrops of woodland, mountain, or desert. Every time you go, you'll find something new to notice: a bug on the forest floor, an inconspicuous bird perched on a branch to the side.

Every family that visits arrives at its favorites. Here are some of ours: the meteorites and the moon rock, the Haida canoe in the 77th Street foyer, the Barosaurus rearing up to protect

her child at the Central Park West entrance, the birds and reptiles. The IMAX theater is pleasantly luxurious, with comfy seats (but no 3-D glasses). The family programs are extensive (call to find out). Before you leave, stand for a moment at the entrance to the Hall of Ocean Life and listen to the response as people first catch sight of the vast blue whale suspended in dark blue light. After a period of thunderstruck awe, they notice that there are little tables down there under the whale. What a place to stop for some chocolate milk and a foot-long hot dog!

American Museum of the Moving Image

3601 35th Avenue bet. 36th and 37th Sts., Astoria, Queens
718-784-0077
www.ammi.org
Closed: Mondays

Ages: 5 and up

Getting there:
G or R to
Steinway
Street

Approach the spanking-white American Museum of the Moving Image on a sunny day, and it looks like L.A. Fortunately, you're in Astoria, which is easier to reach. There is much knowledge and kitsch on display here, from interactive exhibits that will hook you as much as they do the kids, to large displays of movie memorabilia of all sorts.

S tart at the third floor, where the "Behind the Screen" exhibit expertly demonstrates how movies work. An extraordinary moving sculpture called *Feral Fount* employs a strobe to achieve a surreal optical illusion. *Now You See It* consists of two abstract paintings mounted on opposite sides of a rotating panel to spell out the work's title, as clear a demonstration of the way animation works as you'll see. Farther along are computer stations where you can create a cartoon, videotape yourself for a flip-book you can buy at the gift shop, or edit special effects and sound. We liked replacing the sound of a crash sequence from *The Terminator* with squawking chickens.

O n the second floor you'll see more of what goes on in front of the camera. On the Monk's Cafe set from "Seinfeld," even the napkin dispensers are authentic. You can see Robin Williams's fat suit from *Mrs. Doubtfire* and Marlon

Brando's bite plate from *The Godfather*. A wonderful photo sequence shows the 31-year-old Dustin Hoffman getting made up to play 121 in *Little Big Man*. Kids will enjoy the substantial *Star Wars* presence: merchandise, costume and makeup elements, even the Yoda puppet from *The Empire Strikes Back*. Many of the other relics, however, like the Howdy Doody Night Light and the Eve Arden Coloring Book, will probably leave the kids nonplused.

Whatever you do, don't miss the ground-floor Tut's Movie Palace, a tiny (30-seat), ornate Egyptian-style movie palace designed by Red Grooms, where kids can watch movie serials from the Golden Age surrounded by Grooms's antic imaginings. Check out the mummified Tut who pops up out of his sarcophagus, and a fake candy concession offering Luxor Liks and Tut's Nuts. While the children are at the show, parents can salivate by the TV-dinner display.

Call before you visit, because the absolute highlight of any visit here is sometimes in storage. This is the hands-on video-game exhibit on the first floor. They're all here: heavyweights Donkey Kong, Pac-Man, and Pong, cult classics like Karate Champ, Pole Position, and Space Invaders, and even an assortment of PC and console games. Most are in working order, and each has a card explaining its role in the saga of computer-operated entertainment. Bring lots of change, and spend it here.

Bronx Museum of the Arts

1040 Grand Concourse at 165th Street, Bronx
718-681-6000
www.fieldtrip.com/ny/86816000.htm
Closed: Mondays, Tuesdays

Ages: 5 and up

Getting there: C, D, or 4 train to 161st Street/River Avenue

Just a few blocks north of Yankee Stadium and a world away from the boutique galleries of SoHo, the Bronx Museum of the Arts displays work that is ferociously smart, urgent, and compelling. Only a portion of the museum's holdings is on show at any given time, but the temporary exhibitions are so vivid, so interesting, that you won't be disappointed, no matter when you come.

Walk into this immaculate, light-filled modern building, and you'll be struck by how much of the work conveys a powerful sense of place. Most of the artists are of Asian, Latin American or African descent; their work is often highly political and always relevant to the community of the Bronx. When we visited, we saw, in an exhibition called "Urban Mythologies," warm and affectionate plaster life casts of people in the community, bold, intelligent canvases by the children of Tim Rollins's K.O.S (Kids of Survival) group, and many multimedia installations. One was called *The Last Farm in the Bronx,* and it featured maps, photographs, wooden cutouts of figures and a pair of Chinese slippers for wearing while walking around the maps. Two neat rows of three-inch wooden blocks had English words carved into them; they were made on long subway trips by a Korean artist, recently arrived in the city and trying to teach himself English. Chances are you'll see something involving graffiti, something involving video. You'll get the message: These artists are preoccupied with the individual's place in society. It's not a hard message for kids, so deeply concerned with safety and a sense of belonging, to understand.

Call to find out about special programs, workshops for older children (in art, computer graphics, film animation, and lots more), and celebrations. The monthly Family Sundays give your children the chance to look thoughtfully at the art on display and then make their own.

Brooklyn Children's Museum

145 Brooklyn Avenue at St. Mark's Avenue, Crown Heights, Brooklyn
718-735-4400
www.bchildmus.org
Closed: Mondays, Tuesdays

Ages: Up to 8

Getting there: 3 or A to Kingston Street, 2 to President Street

The Brooklyn Children's Museum is a true pioneer, the oldest children's museum in the country and the inspiration for hundreds that have followed. Its mission, pursued for a hundred years, is nothing less than to teach children how to look at the world. But that's not why you want to come here. You want to come here because your kids, especially the under-8s, will have a great time, and you will get to bask in the self-satisfied glow that comes from surviving an environment so profoundly kid-centric that you will be hard pressed to find a chair big enough to sit in.

This is a kids' world. The building is mostly underground, and once inside you face an enormous, red-lit tunnel made out of a corrugated drainage duct, which slopes down to the museum's main level. Alongside your path runs a shallow stream of water in which kids will find paddle wheels, ramps, and stones to manipulate. Rooms and passageways branch off the tunnel, so your visit can be orderly, starting from the bottom and working up, or—as most kids seem to prefer—helter-skelter.

Every exhibit has a participatory element. In the music area you'll find thumb pianos and assorted percussion instruments, but the star of the show is a row of "piano keys" on the floor that you jump on to produce notes, the way Tom Hanks did in *Big*. In "The City" you can decorate a float, make a (fabric) pizza, or play New York street games. Pick up a plant in the greenhouse and run experiments on it; build a giant insect out of foam-rubber parts. There's a play area just for under-6s, which is full of soft toys, blocks and costumes, and which always seems to be full of over-stimulated kids recovering themselves with a little normal play, while their glassy-eyed parents look on.

On the top floor, older kids—say, up to 8 or 9—will enjoy "The Mystery of Things," a marvelously thoughtful exhibit about the ways we perceive and use objects. A huge case full of shoes of every description, and another of spoons, are the winners. Adults will get a kick out of the small display of objects from the museum's early days: a stuffed, mounted ermine posed in an attitude of combat; fist-sized models of flies, which open up to reveal the insects' interiors.

A mong the many weekend special events, you may encounter snake-feeding demonstrations, storytelling, and the occasional show in the Tank Theater, a charming little amphitheater made out of an old corn-oil vat. Several of these events are specifically for children under 5. During vacation time, there are many special programs and the museum stays open for extended hours. The small gift shop has reasonably priced things that kids will want. Our favorite is the slim volume of belly-button tattoos for a dollar.

B rooklyn Museum of Art

200 Eastern Parkway, Prospect Heights, Brooklyn
718-638-5000
www.brooklynart.org
Closed: Mondays, Tuesdays, Thanksgiving, Christmas Day, New Year's Day

All ages

Getting there: 2 or 3 to Eastern Parkway/ Brooklyn Museum

I f the Brooklyn Museum of Art were in another city, it would be a major attraction for tourists and local culture vultures alike. Its world-class assemblages (especially Egyptian, African, and Native American) constitute the nation's second-largest collection of art, and they're housed in a big Beaux Arts pile that looks just the way a world-class museum should—grand and looming. The BMA has its own subway stop and a big parking lot, and it's next-door to the superb Brooklyn Botanic Garden. But even with all this going for it, the museum is rarely crowded. The Brooklyn aspect seems to deter many tourists and ladies who lunch. This is a source of never-ending frustration for the museum's officials, but for you and your little ones, it makes for a stress-free cultural experience.

As you enter the Grand Lobby, look out for whatever extravagant installation is in residence. It's likely to be strange and interesting. First stop? Try the period rooms on the fourth floor; kids love to peek into furnished rooms of the past, and each room has an exquisite tiny model of the house it came from right next to it. Don't miss the ornate Victorian parlor, where a long double line of wooden animals winds across the floor to a Noah's Ark; the scene is watched over by a mysterious figure, a little  girl with ringlets who sits perpetually facing away from her twentieth-century visitors.

Next, the Egyptian collection on the third floor; that shadowy-looking mummy is real! And there's a wonderful gold ibis which has become the museum's unofficial mascot. Then down to the ground floor, with its towering totem poles, spooky masks, and New World artifacts. The museum calls them "Primitive Art"; it seems an incongruous label for these exquisite objects.

There's more, enough to fuel many visits. Here are a few of our picks: the outsize female nude by Lachaise on the fifth floor is always good for a shocked giggle. Thomas Cole's heroic Catskill landscapes are full of details that will fascinate the kids, as will a portrait of George Washington looking much younger than you've ever imagined him. The Decorative Arts section makes you look at vacuum cleaners, steam irons, and chairs with fresh eyes. And right off the Asian and Oriental galleries on the second floor is a mezzanine devoted to recent acquisitions. You can walk by a vitrine of Islamic pottery, turn a corner, and find yourself staring at a Chuck Close portrait—eye-opening, no matter what your age.

There are two well-stocked gift shops, one especially for kids (see page 149). If you're hungry, try the pretty, light-filled cafeteria on the first floor, which offers decent food. Or dine alfresco next door at the Brooklyn Botanic Garden, or cross Eastern Parkway and head down Washington Avenue to the legendary, kid-friendly, Tom's Restaurant.

The BMA has a fabulously successful event on the first Saturday evening of each month, when the museum is open until 11 P.M. and admission is free after 6 P.M. The "First Saturday" roster includes a movie, dancing to live music in the great hall, and arty, exciting entertainment for the kids. If you go, be prepared. This normally tranquil place will be positively bursting with people and buzz.

N.B. In the summer, a free shuttle bus runs between the garden and the other cultural institutions in the neighborhood.

Children's Museum of Manhattan

212 West 83rd Street
bet. Broadway and Amsterdam Avenue
212-721-1234
www.cmom.org
Closed: Mondays, Tuesdays

Ages: Up to 8

Getting there:
1, 9, B, or C to
86th Street

Situated in the heart of the Upper West Side, the four-story Children's Museum of Manhattan is interactive from top to bottom. With its cheerful, friendly atmosphere, it's the kind of place parents and baby-sitters are happy to revisit on a rainy day or on those long Sundays when everyone's out of ideas. Grownups may feel a tad limp after a visit, but the kids will have a great time zooming around, and they may even learn something.

The ground-floor "Body Odyssey" is an irresistible place to start. Designed to show the workings of the body, it focuses (naturally) on the yuckier aspects of human physiology. You can crawl through a blood-delivery tube, bombard your best friend with baby blood cells (round red pillows), squirt "digestive juices" at food, look at a video of intestines chugging away, and open a drawer to find a convincing replica of poop. You get the idea. For those interested in quieter pursuits, there are computer stations for playing "Body Battles", and, all around you, questions to be explored: "How is your blood like the subway system?" "What happens to your burger?" (Yes, it's in that drawer...) The sheer ingenuity on show here is undeniable—though, as you watch the kids racing around with large flakes of "skin" (stiff, fabric disks) or pushing "mucus" through giant rubber nose hairs, you have to wonder about the folks who come up with this kind of thing.

Try younger kids on the lower-level Dr. Seuss exhibit, with its wild Seussian structures and doodads. You have to be under 4 to get into "Wordplay", an imaginative play area tucked away on the second floor and subdivided into nooks where you can play kitchen, post

office, or tree house, or simply recline while Mom tickles your tummy and chats with the other moms, all of whom have that grateful look of harried people enjoying a few minutes' respite. One floor up, in the supervised Early Childhood Center, the little ones can absorb themselves in messy art or play with small toys (balls, trucks, and so on). It's crowded, it's intense, it's noisy. What did you expect?

Meanwhile, older sophisticates have not been overlooked. In the media center on the third floor they can produce and star in TV game shows, panel discussions, and weather and news broadcasts. Those who so choose can be on camera, where giggling and blushing seem to be the norm, but it seems equally inviting to work the cameras and sound effects. When we were there, the sound-effects person caused mild hysteria by being unable to turn off the "thinking music" during a game show.

The modest gift shop carries educational games and art-and-craft stuff, but mementos aren't the point of this museum; being there is.

Children's Museum of the Arts

**182 Lafayette Street,
bet. Broome and Grand Streets
212-274-0986
Closed: Mondays, Tuesdays**

Ages: Up to 8

**Getting there:
6 to Spring
Street**

A large, insouciant zebra marks the entrance to this friendly place. Just off the edge of SoHo is the beautiful new space of the Children's Museum of the Arts, with gleaming wood floors, lofty tin ceilings, lots of pipes, ducts, and ceiling fans, and walls painted with a suave eye for color (that is, not the usual flat, primary colors you see on plastic toys). And there's art everywhere. Look beyond the daubs *du jour* pinned up to dry, and you'll see extraordinary pictures made by children around the world. They're properly framed, too, so you can see how fresh and accomplished they are. They perch alongside works by noted artists (we saw some eye-catching trucks by Peter Sis) and all kinds of work—mobiles, sculptures, collages—by local artists.

CMA nourishes its link to the neighborhood in other ways, offering drop-in programs for local kids (6 months to 4 years) on some weekday mornings, assorted after-school programs (painting on canvas, using papier-mâché, even a Japanese-language art class for Japanese kids!), a "summer art colony," special family events, and so on.

But even if you don't live in SoHo or Chinatown and just show up with your child, he or she can plunge right into art, music, or whatever special activity is going on. Start on the ground floor, settling at one of the companionably spaced easels or tables, all of which are equipped with every kind of drawing and coloring implement, Play-Doh, collage material, and glue. On the outside wall of the "art house," a mustard-colored tower with a winding staircase, you'll find announcements of the day's activities. Inside, slides of artworks and stars are projected on the dark ceiling. A special infant area has a rug, pillows, toys, and books (and, yes, a changing table).

The downstairs is set up for more art as well as fantasy play. The first thing kids will notice is the enclosure that's filled with enormous, very light balls. A little decorous bouncing or catch will get their creative juices flowing, but remember, this ain't McDonald's, and life-threatening behavior is not well received. There's a stage, and a corner where your kids can sit with a musician or storyteller.

This whole place feels creative and bustling, and it has no shortage of imaginative people to help a budding genius realize his or her vision or just have a great time. Keep it in mind the next time you've been shlepping the kids around SoHo and they need a break.

The Cloisters

Fort Tryon Park
bet. 190th and Dyckman Streets
212-923-3700
www.metmuseum.org
Closed: Thanksgiving, Christmas Day,
New Year's Day

All ages

Getting there: By car, drive north on Henry Hudson Parkway. A sign will direct you to the museum's small (medieval, actually) parking lot. By subway, take the A train to 190th Street, leave the station via elevator, and walk up through Fort Tryon Park. By bus, take the M4 to the last stop.

Taking the kids on frequent trips to the Cloisters is one of the great privileges of life in New York. Not that New York kids in particular have a special bent toward medieval art and history. Nor are they fascinated by the fact that the building, with its multiple courtyards and stairways and connecting passages, was assembled on this majestic site from bits and pieces of several real medieval European chapels and cloisters in the 1930s. In fact, no matter how earnestly you explain what a cloistered monastery is, your kids will just think it's a castle, possibly an enchanted one. That is, after all, what it looks like.

I t has an enchanted feel to it, too, sitting in splendid isolation at the end of a winding cobblestone drive atop Fort Tryon Park. But the collection itself can present a problem. Medieval art is almost entirely religious, full of conventions and symbols that are foreign to most modern kids. So, once you arrive, head directly for the astounding Unicorn Tapestries. This is as close as fabric will ever get to behaving like film. The movement, drama, and mystery of this woven narrative crosses generations effortlessly.

T here's more: the knights' sarcophagi. Point out that these tombs actually contained dead knights, and you may be rewarded with a satisfying shudder. In the Treasury, seek out our favorite item—the sixteenth-century rosary bead carved from box-

wood. The size of a walnut, it opens like a locket, and has panels inside that unfold to form a triptych depicting scenes from the life of Christ. The detail is incredible—literally hundreds of minute figures are carved into this bead, with facial expressions, fingernails, and hair. The precious-metal pieces are worked almost as elaborately. If it's a bright day, the light coming through the plentiful stained glass looks jeweled.

Next, stroll around the enclosed gardens, the cloisters themselves. If you hear the soft sound of monks chanting, you're not hallucinating. Recorded music is played several times a day, and even the youngest kids pick up the contemplative vibe—until they realize that the bare stone rooms and gloomy staircases right off the gardens are perfect for a quick round of fantasy play. Don't leave without going out onto the parapet, with its brilliant river views. You may begin to think you're in a castle, too.

Pick up a unicorn postcard on the way out, and, if you have the time, take a leisurely bus ride home. The M4 runs from the Cloisters down upper Broadway, then east on 110th Street and on down Fifth. Stare out the windows at the absorbing, changing cityscape before you. For the price of a fare, you get a show.

Dyckman Farmhouse Museum

4881 Broadway at 204th Street
212-304-9422
www.preserve.org/hht/hht.htm
Closed: Mondays

All ages

Getting there:
A, 1 or 9 to
207th Street

The most amazing thing about the Dyckman Farmhouse is its very existence. More than 200 years old, Manhattan's only surviving Dutch farmhouse stands in its leafy garden, surrounded by the urban bustle, traffic, and apartment buildings of upper Broadway. Don't expect a stately place with a lot of splendid silverware; the charm of Dyckman is more rough-hewn. When you clamber up the steps and inside, you'll find two rooms of note. The Relic Room has munitions, uniforms, and Hessian crockery. A Revolutionary War–era musket that belonged to the family has recently been returned by a descendant. In the kitchen, the huge, sturdy cooking implements and the open hearth look

straight out of the Brothers Grimm. Through the kitchen window, you'll see scratchings in the rock that represent a playing board for Nine Man's Morris (What else? See page 62), an eighteenth-century children's game.

On summer Saturday afternoons you can sit on the recently restored back porch and sample old-timey activities: churn butter, dip candles, spin wool. Now, this kind of thing makes many parents jittery, and, to tell the truth, there's an awful lot of it around. But this is the only Manhattan venue for such ancient crafts, and it wouldn't hurt anybody to try, at least once.

Here's an approach. Set aside an hour or so for the Dyckman, then visit Carrot Top Pastries, a local institution (5025 Broadway at 214th Street) that serves sandwiches and legendary carrot cake. The other great local attraction is Inwood Hill Park, like the farmhouse a survivor: the last original woodland on Manhattan Island. It has cliffs, voles, sweeping views of the Hudson and the Palisades, many, many kinds of birds and trees, and, up a steep hill, the justly famous Indian caves. Native Americans did indeed inhabit these sheltered niches under big, jutting rock ledges, and the noises of the city seem to fade away as you squat in the cool, dim spaces. Ask a Park Ranger, or stop in at the park's Urban Ecology Center for directions.

Ellis Island Immigration Museum

Ellis Island (in New York Harbor)
212-363-3200
www.ellisisland.org
Open: Daily

Ages: 8 and up

Getting there:
1 or 9 to South
Ferry; 4 or 5
to Bowling
Green, ferry
to the island
via Statue of
Liberty (buy
tickets at
Castle
Clinton)

This landmark has deep reso-
nance for those whose ancestors
were among the millions
received and processed here; for others,
it represents a stirring chapter of the
American story.

For children without a family connection or
some knowledge of the history, though, Ellis
Island can be a little daunting. Bring them at
an age when they can read comfortably—it's the
poignant quotations and letters accompanying the
mostly black-and-white photographic displays that
bring the story home. And if you have a choice,
don't do Ellis Island and the Statue of Liberty as a
package. Although the same ticket gets you into
both, together they're more than the average kid
can handle.

In this majestic building's abandoned days and
before its sensitive restoration, the ghosts here
must have been easily sensed. Now the best way
to feel them is to visit the photographic exhibit

called "Silent Voices" on the third floor, where you'll see pictures of the place as it was left, with rows of iron beds, their mattresses neatly rolled, long tables with a soup bowl and spoon at each place, and, in glass cases, heaps of dusty, rusty relics, from cooking pots and crutches to office typewriters and fans. The children's favorites on this top floor will be in "Treasures from Home," a display of immigrants' precious possessions. Amid framed photos and family Bibles, you'll find small dolls and teddy bears, featherbeds, handmade patterned clothes, and English clogs.

The second-floor Registry Room is imposing, high-ceilinged, and empty but for a few rows of wooden benches. It has a pronounced echo, as children tend to discover quickly. At the West End is a clutter of little rooms, tiled and painted a rich, institutional yellow. Here you'll find the best exhibit, "Through America's Gate," which details every step of the tortuous process the immigrants had to undergo before they were allowed in (or, in some sad cases, deported). Talk the kids through it; tell them about the six-second medical inspections and the letters that got chalked onto people's coats (E for eyes).

Show them the apparatus for "mental testing", stop to read aloud the harrowing words of the new arrivals. Peer in at the reconstructed Hearing Room, and don't miss the preserved graffiti.

Depending on how much stamina and interest your children have, show them either the East End exhibit, "Peak Immigration Years" (lots of fabulous photographs), or take a turn on the ground floor, which has an elaborate display of immigration statistics. Be warned, though: To many youngsters (and plenty of parents too), the block graphs and ranks of numbers are dry and academic. Instead, make a beeline for the enormous globe with trails of lights showing patterns of world migrations from 1700 on (English going to Australia, Chinese to Indonesia, slaves to America). There's also an ethnic map of America here; Press a button and learn the size of any ethnic population currently living in any state in the country. (Another option: the moving documentary called *Island of Hope, Island of Tears,* which shows continuously throughout the day.)

The cafeteria serves an array of international fast foods, from pizza and nachos to gyro sandwiches and tuna on croissant. At the tasteful gift shop you can find candy of many lands in among the usual bookmarks, fridge magnets, and folk-art items.

Forbes Magazine Galleries

62 Fifth Avenue, cor. 12th Street
212-206-5548
Closed: Mondays, Thursdays, Sundays

All ages

Getting there:
D, F, or Q to
14th Street

This place is a joy. Publisher and bon vivant Malcolm Forbes never saw the need to put away childish things; on the contrary, he collected and cherished them. Much of his collection is on show here—toy soldiers, Fabergé eggs, presidential memorabilia, and more, gathered in an eccentric, endearing museum that's just compact enough to keep even very young kids interested.

The first gallery contains 500 toy ships and boats of all sizes and degrees of complexity, deployed on gleaming glass seas. All around, you hear jolly nautical band music and the booming of ships' horns. The submarine display is the star of the show; the sub floats murkily behind a long, vertical window, you hear the ominous beeping of depth finders, and suddenly you notice a model of the *Lusitania*, sprawled on the bottom.

41

In the next gallery, thousands and thousands of toy soldiers and other figures are arranged in tiny, elaborate tableaux. You can see a pitched battle between Aztecs and Cortés's conquistadores, tiny wounded men lying in field hospitals, Indians on a moving belt that slowly circles the wagon trains, and regiment after regiment marching on parade. (Be warned; some of these displays are, incomprehensibly, too high up for children under the age of, say, 8, so you may have to hoist them up from time to time, or locate the stools that are usually somewhere around.) Don't miss the scene of William Tell preparing to shoot the apple from his son's head. Peer through a little porthole-shaped window in a room called Land of Counterpane, and you can pretend to be the child of Robert Louis Stevenson's poem, lying in bed with all your soldiers laid out in formation on the quilt in front of you.

That's not all. The section of presidential memorabilia has Abraham Lincoln's actual stovepipe hat, the eyeglasses he dropped when he was shot, and his handwritten copy of the Gettysburg Address. There are also some of JFK's jottings that Caroline scrawled on. Last, the Fabergé room, which, though it's more enthralling for adults, has aspects that children too will find fascinating: the miniaturization and the surprises, such as hens, tucked away inside the 13 gorgeous eggs made for the czars.

Fort Wadsworth, Gateway National Recreation Area

New York Avenue, Staten Island
718-354-4500
www.nps.gov
Closed: Mondays, Tuesdays

All ages

Getting there: By car, cross the Verrazzano-Narrows Bridge, lower level, take the Bay Street exit, turn right, and keep going. By ferry and bus: Take the Staten Island Ferry, then the S51 bus

Cross the soaring Verrazano-Narrows Bridge from Brooklyn to Staten Island, and far below you, at the foot of the Staten Island end, there's a fort. One of the oldest military installations in the country, and certainly one of the most exciting to visit, Fort Wadsworth is the perfect mix of crumbly, atmospheric ruin and imposing stone fortifications, with an astounding view of New York Harbor and Manhattan, and grassy, breezy hillsides where everyone can decompress while inhaling the stiff sea breezes.

For years the fort was an abandoned ruin; its restoration began once it became part of the National Parks System, in 1995. Today most of the 220-acre site is open to visitors. You and yours are free to scramble around on your own, checking out the abandoned gun turrets half-hidden in the undergrowth, but it's also well worth attaching yourselves to a guided tour (call for times); you'll be able to see things that are off-limits to the casual explorer.

43

Wadsworth was part of New York's complex defense system for a hundred years, from the mid-nineteenth century. Unlike Fort Hamilton, its counterpart across the water in Bay Ridge, Wadsworth has no soldiers on the premises but makes up for that with cool stuff. The oldest building is the massive Battery Weed, which was begun in 1847. Right at the water's edge, it's a looming stone structure with three levels of cannon-ports (space for 116 of the big guns) and impressive echoes. The guide will explain how cannons worked in a way that you can all understand, and if you're a game-looking crowd he'll lead you off to see the nineteenth-century latrine and make ghoulish jokes for the kids. Supposedly many hidden tunnels and passageways between the gun emplacements still exist.

On top of the hill sits Fort Tompkins, the barracks, where about 700 soldiers were billeted. Here, you'll thread your way through so many identical, vaulted-brick passageways that you'll feel as if you're in a maze. This seemingly impregnable place has two sets of walls (the granite outer walls are 30 feet thick) with a space in between where attackers could be trapped in a crossfire; the guard will point out that rifle slits in each wall are "offset," that is, not placed directly opposite each other, to minimize the risk of a comrade's being shot by accident. This is a kid-friendly fact. Our guide (who told us, quite persuasively, that he was a Scottish nobleman called Sir John Wemyss-Kessler) encouraged us to linger in the pitch-black gunpowder-storage room which contains a ghost named George. Fortunately, George was shy.

Save some time after the tour for exploring; you'll find surprises along the trails—an observation post with a rusty phone installation from which the officers could track cannon fire and phone in course corrections; the burned-out railhead where mines and torpedoes were unloaded. If you go in the spring, wildflowers will be blooming in the woods. Bring a picnic.

N.B. The Fort Wadsworth Visitor Center is open Wednesday through Sunday from 10 A.M. to 5 P.M.

One Block
4
Museums

Broadway bet. Houston and Prince Streets

Guggenheim Museum SoHo

575 Broadway
212-423-3500
www.guggenheim.org
Closed: Mondays, Tuesdays
All ages

New Museum of Contemporary Art

583 Broadway
212-219-1222
www.newmuseum.org
Closed: Mondays, Tuesdays
All ages

Anne Frank Center U.S.A.

584 Broadway, Suite 408
212-431-7993
http://www.annefrank.com/afc/center1.html
Closed: Saturday through Monday,
from June 1 through August 31
Saturday and Sunday from September 1 through May 31
Ages: 9 and up

Museum for African Art

593 Broadway
212-966-1313
www.africanart.org
Closed: Mondays
All ages

Here's an outing made for one afternoon and several sets of interests, not the least of which is the parents' desire for pricey artisanal bread or some such from Dean and Deluca. Everyone can be happy with a quick stop in at least two of these museums. The Guggenheim's lovely, two-story loft space is immediately attractive, and past exhibitions have been multimedia, using

all kinds of interesting materials, from styrofoam to neon. (Once we saw some gorgeous work there made entirely out of vegetation, including what looked like a whole shrubbery.) Currently, the whole second floor is occupied by Andy Warhol's *The Last Supper,* which consists of many variations on Leonardo da Vinci's monumental work. The New Museum is always interesting, often edgy, with lots of provocative and eye-catching shows, but you have to watch out for explicit images (sexual or violent) and grim subjects (AIDS).

Many New York children appreciate contemporary art with the ease that comes from having seen a lot of it. Contemporary African art is harder to find. Stimulate their eyes at the Museum for African Art. It's sleek and beautiful, designed by Maya Lin (architect of the Vietnam Veterans Memorial in Washington, D.C.) and its shows change every six months. The mix of work—ritual objects and painting, jewelry and masks, both traditional and contemporary—will give you a hint as to the richness and variety of African cultures. If you live nearby or visit SoHo often, take a look at the extraordinary special events that are available for children and families.

Finally, the Anne Frank Center U.S.A. tells its heartbreaking story through pictures, words and artifacts. A series of illustrated panels skillfully relates the travails of the Frank family to the larger history of the 30s and 40s. The illustrations include archival pictures of the time (a young Hitler saluting his followers, Depression-era German kids playing with blocks made of near-worthless currency) as well as snapshots of the Franks. Also on display are vintage items (Nazi propaganda posters, cloth stars), some Frank-family mementos (letters from Otto, homework by Margot), and a large, detailed model of the house into which Anne and her family disappeared for two years. This modest exhibit puts a human face—the pretty, smiling face of Anne Frank—on a horrific time; it is a most effective and compassionate history lesson to which any kid who's ever felt trapped can relate.

GSolomon R. uggenheim Museum

1071 Fifth Avenue at 89th Street
212-423-3500
www.guggenheim.org
Closed: Thursdays

All ages

Getting there:
4, 5, or 6 to
86th Street

Y ou can question the Guggenheim's merits as an exhibition space, but not as a playground. This world-famous structure designed by Frank Lloyd Wright has put more than one child in mind of a gigantic toilet bowl, the Death Star, or a locale for Jackie Chan's next film. Inside, the space inspires action; this is surely the only museum in New York City that kids will want to race up and roll

down, all the while shouting across the great, coiling rotunda. Even the stairway landings can upstage the art (they're good for hiding). So, if you want your kids to look at the exhibits properly, don't start at the top, which presents an irresistible downward slope. Instead, conduct your tour in a stately way, uphill. There is always

49

the chance, of course, that your children will never forgive you for this and will become philistines out of spite.

Most of the Guggenheim's space is devoted to temporary exhibitions (call ahead to check for appropriateness), but the Thannhauser Gallery, off the rotunda, houses the museum's core collection of late-nineteenth- and early-twentieth-century art. These paintings are easy to love: Pissarro landscapes, Degas dancers, a Monet view of Venice, moody van Goghs, lush Tahitian scenes by Gauguin. The colorful, playful Kandinskys appeal particularly to children, and so do the works of Léger, whose large Cubist works, like *La Grande Parade,* have a curvy, roly-poly quality that's quite at odds with the more geometric, severe Picassos nearby. If the kids respond to the Cubist works, be sure to point out the almost abstract Cézanne still lifes. And whatever you do, don't miss the dreamy, fairy-tale-like Chagalls, especially the haunting *Green Violinist;* he's the original fiddler on the roof.

Perhaps because of the Guggenheim's unique physical plant, its staff projects a quality of having seen everything that can possibly be seen in a museum. Nothing, but nothing, fazes them. As long as you *don't* touch the art, they are pleasant and helpful.

The cafeteria is small and pleasantly decorated, in a sort of swooping, "Jetsons"-like futuristic style. The food is modest (sandwiches,

Yoo-Hoo, *beer and wine*) and only slightly pricey, and you sit surrounded by pictures of famous artists and the museum itself under construction. Our favorite items in the gift shop were the miniature Eames chairs, but they cost almost as much as the real thing. More reasonable are Babar pens, metal Parlor Puzzlers, cute paste jewelry, and Keith Haring pull toys.

Historic Richmond Town

441 Clarke Avenue bet. Richmond Road and Arthur Kill Road, Staten Island
718-351-1617
Closed: Mondays, Tuesdays

All ages

Getting there: Staten Island Ferry to S74 bus

New York's answer to Colonial Williamsburg, Virginia, Historic Richmond Town contains 27 houses in various stages of restoration spread over what was once the provincial heart of Staten Island. Unlike Williamsburg, though, Richmond Town is just a stone's throw from the modern world, and that's part of its charm. It has a timeless atmosphere, which steals over you as you stroll among the little houses, watching your kids engage in such traditional activities as rolling down a grassy hill or jumping on and off stoops.

During the summer months most of the buildings are open, and friendly locals in period dress promenade in the streets, sit in front parlors, and demonstrate traditional crafts and trades such as tinsmithing and woodworking. These buffs have a gravity and poise that makes them more believable than you'd think—whether despite or because of the distinctly unColonial NooYawk accents, it's impossible to say.

But Richmond Town is at its best for special events. Old Home Day, an autumn extravaganza, is held on the third Sunday in October. The buffs are out in force. A gent in buckskins demonstrates the action on a muzzle-loading rifle he seems to have built by himself, or at least been heavily involved with. These folks all seem to have a real knowledge of their specialties. You can buy hearth-prepared soup, bread, and sarsparilla at the tavern, right near the roof-raising-demo site. The Home Brewers of Staten Island are permitted to sell their root beer but not their more serious beverages,

alas. They'll give you a little cup of beer, porter, or stout for free, though. There are buggy rides, games and a huge mound of hay for kids to jump into, and live music on the vertiginous steps of the Greek Revival Third County Courthouse. As the light starts to fade, mosey down to the gristmill and watch it make grist, then see whether there are any ducks left on the pond behind.

For the annual Train Festival in June, a huge and varied Lionel train layout fills most of the second floor of the courthouse. The display, an all-American landscape of mountains, villages, cities, and farms, is the creation of the Staten Island Track Pack, whose members will happily answer your questions when they are not tending to the trains. Vendors sell model trains (new and prewar) and indispensable accessories, so bring money. If you go, be warned; Many of the houses will be closed up (everything opens for the summer season at the end of the month and stays open until Labor Day), but it's still pleasant to walk around.

Intrepid Sea-Air-Space Museum

Hudson River/Twelfth Avenue and West 46th Street
212-245-0072
www.intrepid-museum.com
Open: Daily in the summer, closed Mondays and Tuesdays from October through April

All ages

Getting there: By subway, A, C, or E to 42nd Street, then M42 bus west to 42nd Street and Twelfth Avenue, then walk north

A trip to the *Intrepid* makes for a full-size afternoon. At any given time, there's a small flotilla of ships parked here, and they look daunting, so you might be tempted to try the Circle Line Tour, which embarks nearby. Resist—unless your kid is up for three hours on a boat listening to somebody talk—and take heart; this is a thrilling outing.

The museum occupies six retired naval craft, ranging from an old harbor tug to the *Intrepid* itself, an aircraft carrier that served in the Second World War and Vietnam and was also for a time NASA's "prime recovery vessel." Begin your tour on the *Intrepid's* huge hangar deck. Ancient military planes and battered space capsules dangle from the ceiling; the kids will make a beeline for the genuine fighter-plane cockpit (it's hard to see how anyone larger than a child could sit in it, actually). Much of the space is devoted to the *Intrepid's* part in World War II, with intricate table models of some of the ship's big engagements. They have the appeal of toys but are, fortunately, under glass. Your kids will be thrilled by the details: A Japanese airplane smaller than your finger tries to escape the great ship, but it trails a wispy cloud of cotton smoke, indicating that it's been hit. Nearby, a bathosphere jockeys for attention with the Thrill Simulator, a ride that rotates passengers upside down and sideways simultaneously. This may be the way astronauts train, but not right after lunch. You can get a dog tag stamped for you while you wait. They cost $5 and up depending on the metal (go for the plain Armed Forces Issue), and they're irresistible.

Before you move on, find the plaque marking the spot where a kamikaze plane hit the ship, killing 10 men. (A total of 99 crewmen were killed during the war, in four separate kamikaze attacks.) When you get to the words "You are standing on hallowed ground," you'll be moved by the gravity of the place.

Clamber up onto the bridge, where weather-beaten retired sailors will explain what all the buttons and switches do. Below decks, you'll find tableaux of life-size mannequins in atmospheric settings, done with a real sense of theater. A group in one cramped room plots coordinates for the guns. Half-filled coffee cups, ashtrays and moody lighting heighten the drama (and might frighten the youngest kids). The explanations accompanying these exhibits are unusually well written, especially those of the U2 spy-plane scandal and the capacity of helicopters to take off and land vertically.

On the wide, breezy flight deck you'll see an array of planes and helicopters. These are the real thing, so if your children should remark that the lethal-looking *Blackbird* reminds them of *Star Wars,* point out that it is in fact the fastest plane in the world.

Before leaving the carrier, walk right to the end of the deck and look north. Nestled under the New York pier of the George Washington Bridge is the Little Red Lighthouse, on which the famous children's story was based; this is one of the few shore views of the little landmark. On any weekend between April and October, you might find yourself staring right at a cruise ship berthed next door at the Passenger Ship Terminals, readying for embarkation. You might even see a load of departing pleasure-seekers in life jackets, gamely practising a life-boat drill.

If you're over 6 and you can fit through the small hatchway at its entrance, you *must* join the (relatively fast-moving) line to enter the nuclear sub *Growler,* the only guided-missile submarine in the world that's open to the public. Minute and claustrophobic (especially the galley and the showers), it can accommodate only 17 visitors at a time. The other boats are interesting enough and well-stocked with talkative old salts, too.

Finally, if you have $5 per child to spare, you might let them tackle the new Navy Flight Simulator, where you pretend you're the pilot of an F18 taking off from the deck of an aircraft carrier somewhere in the Persian Gulf to engage enemy craft. Alternatively, if energies are flagging, you might spend the money at the cute and funky Cupcake Cafe (on Ninth Avenue at 39th Street), which is justifiably famous for its you-know-whats and also for its muffins, doughnuts and cookies.

Jewish Museum

1109 Fifth Avenue (entrance on 92nd St.)
212-423-3230
www.thejewishmuseum.org
Closed: Fridays, Saturdays,
major Jewish holidays

Ages: 8 and up

Getting there:
4, 5, or 6 to
86th Street

The 1908 Warburg Mansion is a suitably imposing home for this sprawling collection of Jewish art and artifacts. Much of the space is devoted to the temporary exhibitions, on subjects from Freud to Seinfeld, that have earned the museum its reputation for iconoclasm and rigor. But on the fourth floor you'll find "Pickles and Pomegranates: Jewish Homes Near and Far," an interactive family display that addresses the question "How have the Jews survived as a distinct culture?" in a way that children can get their minds (and hands) around.

Two rooms are set up in the style of 1897. The first belongs to Sarah, an immigrant child living on the Lower East Side; the other to Rafi, a Persian boy. In Sarah's "apartment" are clothes to try on, silverware for setting the table, and a suitcase full of toys of the time. Another case contains the precious things Sarah's mother allowed her to bring to America; kids can choose the treasures they'd pick. All around are photographs (wonderful images by Jacob Riis and Lewis Hine), household objects, the wallpaper and tchotchkes of another time. Before leaving, pick up the wall-mounted handset and listen to Sarah's dad tell bedtime stories.

Next door in Rafi's Persian home, you'll find no chairs, only carpets and cushions. Rafi is excited about his sister's forthcoming marriage, so there are Persian-style wedding outfits to try on. Scattered around are pens and paper for designing your own amulet (Rafi wears one; it is, one assumes, a mezuzah) or tiled wall patterns, and a Mancala-like board game called Ur. Inside a couple of cozy nooks just large enough for a child to clamber into you'll hear Persian music coming from little speakers embedded in the walls.

The rest of the permanent exhibition is dense, and few kids will have the patience to explore the difference between temples and synagogues or the roots of Zionism. Among the appealing treasures are a model of the Temple in a bottle and a battered, pre-Christian-era helmet. (In a

nod to younger visitors, a sign shows a recently clobbered warrior and asks, "How do you think it got dented?") The Interactive Talmud allows you to sit at a computer and sample rabbinical reasoning on such questions as: when is it proper to give food to a beggar? The kosher slaughtering implements will make you grimace; the circumcision sets will make you wince. And some of the artifacts will amaze. Who knew there were Jews in Alaska? As a 1910 Jewish New Year's greeting carved on a piece of walrus tusk shows, there were.

Look for the menorah made of little Statues of Liberty sitting on a Stars-and-Stripes pedestal, an Israeli greeting card depicting Elvis, a mezuzah carried into space by the Jewish astronaut Jeffrey Hoffman in 1985, and of course, the Holocaust mementos, set off discreetly in a small gallery by themselves: a uniform, a spoon, some papers. The most affecting evocation of that time is George Segal's sculpture *The Holocaust,* displayed austerely in a dim alcove: a mound of white, mannequin-like bodies lies in a pool of soft light, while in the foreground a lone figure stands, gripping a strand of barbed-wire fence and looking out at nothing. Anyone old enough to know what this represents will be moved.

There's light, kosher food in Cafe Weissman downstairs, and in the Cooper gift shop on the main floor you'll find the six-pointed Star of David Slinky and the Sigmund Freud fridge magnet, which plays "Try to Remember" when you press it.

Lefferts Homestead Historic House Children's Museum

Flatbush Avenue nr. Empire Boulevard, Prospect Park, Brooklyn
718-965-6505
www.prospectpark.org
Open: Thursday through Sunday; also on Wednesdays in July and August

Ages: Up to 8

Getting there: D or Q to Prospect Park

Location, location, location! This Dutch farmhouse/children's museum is in exactly the right place. Moved in 1918 from its home on Flatbush Avenue, it came to rest in family-friendly Prospect Park, where it sits between the restored carousel and the spankingly renovated zoo. Not surprisingly, many families wander by the old place to sample the crafts, storytelling, games, and assorted quaint activities on offer.

The house itself is a small jewel, with dormer windows and a columned porch, reconstructed in 1783 after British soldiers burned down its seventeenth-century predecessor during the

Revolutionary War. Walk in through the Dutch door, and you'll see parlors opening to left and right off the spacious center hall. The best parlor looks much as you'd expect a best parlor to look—formal, tidy, with nothing going on. The double parlor to your right, though, is set up with kids' toys and games and a dollhouse. This may be your chance to come to grips (finally!) with that staple interactive feature of New York's restored eighteenth-century domiciles, the game of Nine Man's Morris. Its board looks like one for checkers or tic-tac-toe; the game, apparently, resembles neither. In the back half there's an exhibit showing everyday Dutch Colonial life, with clunky kitchen utensils and musical instruments that you can handle. Little kids like it here.

Patient and flexible volunteers conduct trips to the upstairs bedroom, set up in the 1830s style, with foot-warmer, four-poster bed, spinning wheel, musket and a 200-year-old Bible. You'll be touched to see how readily they conduct Q & As with even the smallest children. Another touching aspect: the paintings on the upstairs landing that Peter Lefferts, an artist and living descendant of the family, has made, showing the Lenape Indians of the area, the slaves on the property, and the Lefferts family at home. The family, by the way, sold this house to the city for $1.

However tranquil it seems, this place is a veritable hotbed of old-timey goings-on. A casual visitor can roll hoops on the grass, hang out inside the Lenape wigwam, and experiment with all the games. On Sunday afternoons in the summer, you can listen to stories on the porch. Play your cards right, and you can plant crops, learn how to sew, make linsey-woolsey, or (on the right weekend in August) harvest the Farmstead's flax crop. You'd be surprised at how disarming this place can be, even for your resident too-cool-for-Raffi hipsters.

Liberty Science Center

Liberty State Park, 251 Phillip Street, Jersey City, N.J.
201-200-1000
www.lsc.org
Closed: Thanksgiving, Christmas Day

All ages

Getting there: Take the PATH train and bus, an express bus from the Port Authority Bus Terminal, or the ferry from the World Financial Center. Or you can travel by car. Call for information.

This airy, spacious edifice, sitting in its own little park, with killer views of skyline and harbor, takes interactive education to a new level. In fact, Liberty Science Center offers so many kid-friendly, adult-painless, and genuinely interesting things to do that first-time visitors, especially small ones, may be overwhelmed by the bustle. It can be a noisy, overstimulating place. Our solution: Don't even try to cover everything in one trip. You also have to decide where to start: with a movie (IMAX or laser), or one of the regularly scheduled live demonstrations, or the exhibits? Our recommendation: exhibits first, a live demonstration or two second, and a movie when the kids run out of steam.

For once the cliché is true; there really is something for all ages here. Start at the top, on the Environment Floor. Toddlers can play in an area called The Greenhouse, while older siblings struggle across the climbing wall or squirm through the Touch Tunnel. Everybody will get a kick out of the computerized door frame, which tells you your height when you stand in it (and then tells you to move along), the cutaway worm farm, and the exotic insects—if that's what you call these hefty creatures: millipedes the size of snakes, giant prickly stick insects that look like moving branches, the meaty, hissing cockroaches from Madagascar, and an enormous, brown, furry tarantula. Eeeewwww. Decompress in the Estuary/Atmosphere area, where the warty sea robin tooling around in its tank is as scary as it gets.

Down one flight, the Health Floor has an actual EMS vehicle and a genuine smashed-up car but is otherwise rather upstaged by the wonderments hanging in the three-story atrium: the Hoberman Sphere, expanding from four to 18 feet and then going back again to four, the laser art, and the Torsional Wave Ladder. With one tug on the end of this device, you can send a wave up the full height of the ladder; you'll find the part to tug on the lower Invention Floor. Down here there's virtual basketball and virtual soccer, which pit volunteers from the audience against computer-generated opponents, a Perception Maze full of fun-house mirrors and optical illusions, a Formula One car, a flight simulator, and myriad flashy tricks for all.

The IMAX feature changes regularly and is incredibly impressive. However, our resident IMAX authority feels that Liberty should provide spectators with those spooky goggles that create the maximum 3-D effect. You'll get essential fast food at the Laser Light Cafe, which has indoor and outdoor seating with great views. The biggest treat, however, is the spacious lawn, with its wide, gentle incline—ideal for rolling down. And finally, the enormous, treat-filled gift shop awaits you (see page 150).

A caveat: Liberty Science Center is so close to the city via road (under 10 miles) that you may think you can drive there in a flash. *Not necessarily.* It's quite likely that you will sit in endless, tedious, soul-destroying traffic in the Holland Tunnel, where the light is depressing, the air is foul, and you can't get radio reception (if you must drive, bring tapes). In no time you'll be wondering where everything started to go wrong in your life, and the children will be getting carsick. If you find this prospect daunting, choose public transportation.

Lower East Side Tenement Museum

90 Orchard Street cor. Broome Street
212-431-0233
www.wnet.org/tenement
Closed: Mondays

Ages: 5 and up

Getting there:
F to Delancey
Street; B, D,
or Q to Grand
Street

If you're not already familiar with the Lower East Side Tenement Museum, you have a treat in store. Buy your ticket at the Visitor Center at 90 Orchard Street, and the guide will take you over to No. 97, which is an old (1863) tenement walk-up where you can tour three apartments, painstakingly re-created to convey the lives of three families—Gompertz, Rogarshevsky, and Baldizzi—who lived there between the 1870s and the 1930s. With its dark, narrow hallways and cluttered little apartments, this building fairly reeks of history.

For families, there's a wonderful special feature—a 45-minute visit to the Confino apartment. The Sephardic Jewish Confinos arrived from Turkey in 1916, and the guide is costumed in the character of 14-year-old Victoria Confino. She greets you as if you have just arrived off the boat, proudly shows you around the apartment and tells you about the life that awaits you in New York. Kids will be astonished to talk to this charming, vivacious girl who doesn't know about television and is ecstatic to be using a flush toilet instead of an outdoor privy.

Victoria gets them to wind up the Victrola and handle such implements as the "washer agitator." If you're up for it, she'll even teach you the fox-trot. And all along, she's talking about immigrant life on the Lower East Side—school, jobs, health, nickel movies at the nickelodeon, and who sleeps where when 10 people live in a one-bedroom apartment. It's riveting to hear all this firsthand.

Everything about the museum is intelligently planned, from its Web site (where you can click on a little square of wallpaper to reveal the layer beneath, click again to find the next layer down, and so on) to the volunteers, some of them older people who grew up on the Lower East Side and delight in sharing their memories. Parents who enjoy the Confino visit should do the full one-hour tour; some kids might get a kick out of it too. If you're still enthusiastic, return to Orchard Street to watch the documentaries that are shown in the little screening room. The reminiscing old-timers, with their heavy accents, seem right at home in the multiethnic mix of today's Lower East Side—though none of them has any visible piercings.

N.B. It's possible to book your place on a tour a day in advance, except for Sundays, which are very busy.

Jacques Marchais Museum of Tibetan Art

338 Lighthouse Avenue, Staten Island
718-987-3500
www.tibetanmuseum.com
**Open: April through November,
Wednesday through Sunday**

Ages: 5 and up

**Getting there:
1,9, N or R to
Staten Island
ferry; S74 bus
to Lighthouse
Avenue**

Children readily understand Tibet's plight. They can immediately identify with the idea of a small, peaceable nation preyed upon by a large, neighboring bully. Bring them here, and they'll understand what else about that country captures the world's imagination.

Sprawled on a wooded Staten Island hillside, these low stone buildings contain an extraordinary trove of Tibetan objects assembled by Jacqueline Klauber, an actress from the Midwest who harbored a lifelong passion for all things Tibetan and collected her treasures under the male name of Jacques Marchais so that dealers would do business with her. She died without ever having visited Tibet, but in 1991 the Dalai Lama came to her museum, liked what he saw, and blessed it. No wonder, really; the place exudes spirituality.

The museum's main room has a cool stone floor, ornate blue-glass lanterns, and a smell of incense. All around, gleaming in the dim light, you'll see statues of gods and Buddhas, and many carved ritual objects. Take advantage of the guide, who can explain the symbolism of everything in language that children can easily understand. You'll learn what the colors on the pillars represent and why the Buddha of the future has such big feet; you'll be told how to spot a Buddha (by the "bump of wisdom," which looks like a topknot on his head), what all those arms and legs are doing on some of the figures, and why Tibetans saw fit to make drinking cups out of human skulls (yes, there are a couple on display). The crowded altar all along one wall has three levels and many layers of significance.

Everything in this small museum—from the sand mandala to the elaborate wall hangings and the prancing, spirited sculptures (look for Vaishravana, the deity of wealth, with a jewel-spitting mongoose in his grip)—is so full of life and emotion that your kids will take the time to look. When they've had enough, shepherd them outside to the terraced garden, with its fish-ponds and sculptures of baboons and elephants. It's a wonderful place for a picnic.

N.B. The Tibetan Festival is held every October, and it's truly a winner, mostly because of the monks, who sit in the museum in their rust-colored robes and chant for hours, ringing little bells periodically. Get the kids to close their eyes and succumb to the spell. In the garden, they can cut out and color paper mandalas, watch an enthralling puppet show, consult a fortune-teller and buy Tibetan goods (including some great T-shirts). When we say that the food is tempting for all, we speak the truth; even the pickiest will not find fault with the soft flatbread or the mild, savory vegetable dumplings.

Maritime Industry Museum

6 Pennyfield Avenue, Fort Schuyler, Throg's Neck, Bronx
718-409-7218
www.sunymaritime.edu/museum/index.html
Closed: Sundays

All ages

Getting there: By subway, 6 to Westchester Square, then Bx40 bus to Fort Schuyler. For New York Bus Service express bus from Manhattan, call 718-994-5500 for information. The museum's Web site has more information on transportation.

A trip here is like a visit to the souvenir-filled attic of an eccentric seafaring uncle. Fort Schuyler sits on a small promontory, surrounded on three sides by the waters of Long Island Sound and the East River. Directly overhead arches the Throg's Neck Bridge. It's hard to believe that this dramatic place, with its views, sea breezes, and gloomy stone buildings, is within the city limits.

Built in the early nineteenth century to protect New York City against sea attack from the north, Fort Schuyler still has the manicured look of a military base, though it's now the campus of the SUNY Maritime College. These old buildings also house the Maritime Industry Museum, a motley assemblage of miniatures (some of which are enormous), historic prints and paintings, and artifacts of the maritime trades. Don't expect interactivity; this is an old-fashioned, labor-of-love museum where you look but don't touch. Everything is donated, and the signage is often hand-lettered; sometimes there isn't any.

For the methodical, the museum offers a comprehensive history of American ships and shipping. But with kids, you'll have to dodge around in accordance with their whims. Wherever you look, you'll see models, highly detailed replicas of all sorts of vessels, including Cleopatra's barge (complete with a tiny queen of the Nile on deck), a couple of Chinese junks, a Spanish galleon with painted sails, and the doomed luxury liner *Andrea Doria,* with three swimming pools. Look for the small, inconspicuous model of the *St. Mary's,* the first training vessel of the Maritime College; it was made at sea in 1903 by a cadet. Easier to spot are the 10-foot-long models of the *Reliance* and the *Bremen.* These are astoundingly intricate, guaranteed to intrigue collectors of *Star Wars* vehicles or Mighty Max toys. Make sure they notice the tiny pontoon plane parked on the *Bremen's* deck. On the second floor, New York parents will want to study the big (one inch equals 50 feet) model of the Brooklyn

Navy Yard, circa 1940-42. The model contains 273 buildings inside the yard's boundaries, 659 houses and 4 churches outside, 46 naval vessels, 47 mobile cranes, 231 freight cars, and so on. Completion time? Eight years.

The passenger-ship display has menus, ashtrays, wine lists, and pamphlets, including one entitled, "What to Wear on a Grace Line Cruise." Look for the stirring exhibit about the *General Slocum* disaster of 1904, in which more than a thousand people on a Sunday-afternoon outing perished when the paddleboat burst into flame on the East River. No need to linger over the more inscrutable items—the wall of framed Department of Commerce inspectors' licenses, for example, or the unlabeled glass case that contains a length of thick rope pulled through a wooden pulley. (Huh?)

Amenities include soda machines and a gift shop, but if you call in advance when school is in session (roughly, September through May), you can eat in the cafeteria with the cadets. (You know they'll be polite, and we know that the food will be better than in the fast-food places on East Tremont.) In nice weather, bring a picnic and walk down to the water. There's a stone breakwater, a cooking grate, and the occasional fisherman. Gulls squawk overhead. Inhale. Look around. Enjoy.

Metropolitan Museum of Art
Starting Out

1000 Fifth Avenue bet. 80th and 84th St.
212-535-7710
www.metmuseum.org
Closed: Mondays, New Year's Day,
Thanksgiving, and Christmas Day

All ages

Getting there:
4, 5, or 6 to
86th Street

You could spend many happy hours strolling through this enormous repository of world-renowned art, discovering new treasures at every turn. You could, but your kids wouldn't thank you. To make it a successful trip for them, avoid crowds. Don't go when a big-name show has just opened; always arrive early, before the crowds thicken. Also, don't push your luck. Plan your visit in advance; discuss what you'll be seeing. (A wonderful book for children called *Inside the Museum,* by Joy Richardson, is published by the Metropolitan Museum of Art/Harry N. Abrams. Try to get a copy before you go, and the kids will be primed.) Once there, be prepared to move on before the sheer size of the place becomes oppressive.

For those first trips to the Met, nothing beats a ramble around the main (first) floor. We recommend a counterclockwise route, starting out at the Ancient Egyptian galleries, which never fail to enthrall. The ranks of massive sarcophagi are jaw-dropping, while the 23 Meketra models (tiny, industrious clay people found in a tomb and busily at work carting grain, rowing, weaving) will bring delighted smiles. William, the Met's blue-hippo mascot, is somewhere around; ask a guard for directions. Kids' eyes widen at the sight of the Temple of Dendur, especially if they look at the photos of it in situ and grasp the engineering feat that brought it to New York.

Now, a kid-friendly design coup. Behind the temple, though a glass door, there's a selection from the Burdick Collection of baseball trading cards! These delights should sustain you through the American Wing (some great period rooms, but also a whole lot of wardrobes and urns) to the soothing Engelhard Court, an indoor sculpture garden with Louis Comfort Tiffany's exquisite stained glass and mosaic fountain and loggia from his own Long Island home. There are little balconies hidden away at the corners of this beautiful space; to kids they seem like secrets. (Speaking of secrets, see whether they can find the Frank Lloyd Wright room. You'll want to move right in.)

You're just steps away from the massed medieval armor. Its highlights: the armor-clad horses, the child's suit of mail, the assorted pistols, and the ferocious samurai warriors, in suits of steel and leather scales laced together with leather and silk. Here, "awesome" is, for once, the appropriate word.

Now, the home stretch. Don't linger in the Medieval or European Sculpture and Decorative Arts collections. Skip Twentieth-Century Painting; all those Picassos, Cézannes, Monets, Manets, etc. can be attended to on another trip. Press on instead to the Michael C. Rockefeller Wing, which houses the gallery of Asmat art from New Guinea. There's a slender, carved wooden canoe almost 50 feet long, a larger than life-size wooden alligator, and totemlike house posts of wonderful delicacy and mystery.

A quick canter through the Greek and Roman galleries and you're in the gift shop, which is, as you might expect, vast and enticing. (For more about the wonderful children's gift shop, see page 148.) In case anyone's up for it, remember

that the small Costume Institute, one flight down, often has something strange and interesting on view: a shagadelic mini from the 60s, say, or Frederick the Great's enormous shoes. Also on the ground floor, just outside the Uris Center, is a model of the Parthenon that dates from 1889. With its incredible detail, it looks like a huge, lovingly made dollhouse.

Metropolitan Museum of Art
Onward & Upward

Now that your kids are getting comfortable, you can venture upstairs. First stop: Emanuel Gottlieb Leutze's *Washington Crossing the Delaware*. It's the largest painting in the museum and the perfect place to start, because of its heroic scale and subject and also because the artist committed three glaring historical inaccuracies. (If they've looked at *Inside the Museum*, the kids will bring these mistakes to your attention with zeal.) While you're here, you can compare George Washingtons (Gilbert Stuart's portrait is here too) and take in the Edward Hoppers and George Caleb Bingham's *Fur Traders Descending the Missouri*, en route to the European paintings.

Be selective among these riches. Rubens is likely to turn them right off, but the perfect details of rustic life in Brueghel's *The*

Harvesters will hold a kid's interest. So will the Seurats, in their dotty splendor, and most of the other big names: *Cypresses,* by van Gogh, Cézanne's *Card Players.* But be sure you get to this floor's part of the Twentieth-Century galleries, which teem with big, bold, and witty paintings and structures by such notables as O'Keeffe and Paul Klee that will immediately grab the attention of budding connoisseurs. You'll find Grant Wood's *The Midnight Ride of Paul Revere,* and Charles Demuth's sumptuous *The Figure 5 in Gold,* which he painted for poet William Carlos Williams after reading Williams's poem about a fire truck out on a dark night.

For a complete change of pace and tone, stop by the Islamic Art gallery to see pattern upon exquisite pattern, especially in the blue and white niche made of mosaic tile and the pair of gleaming doors carved and inlaid with dodecagons (twelve-sided figures) surrounding twelve-pointed stars. And last, march smartly back to almost the point at which you started, so that you can stand and contemplate the Chinese garden in the Astor Court.

This was here long before the Chinese Scholars Garden in Snug Harbor; it looks as if it's been here for centuries, with its timeless, fantastical rocks, latticed windows, tiled floor, and gentle waterfall. Everything is designed to be looked at from every angle, with the patterns of light changing as you move around. Subtle and mesmerizing, it's the perfect parting vision. Next time the children will choose for themselves.

The Metropolitan offers events and special tours for families and children of different ages. Most are free; a few require reservations. At the Information Desks you can pick up free guides to some of the collections, written especially for young visitors.

El Museo del Barrio

Heckscher Building
1230 Fifth Avenue at 104th Street
212-831-7272
www.elmuseo.org/
elmuseo@aol.com
Closed: Mondays, Tuesdays

All ages

Getting there:
6 to 103rd
Street

In the 30 years since it began—in a public school classroom, then growing into a succession of East Harlem storefronts before finding its present home at the top end of Fifth Avenue's Museum Mile—the Museo del Barrio's scope and purpose have also grown. Originally intended to showcase the art of New York's Puerto Rican community in East Harlem, the museum now holds 8,000 objects, from all over Latin American and the Caribbean, and ranging in date from pre-Columbian to modern

times. Its airy, spacious galleries in the grand, neo-classical Hecksher Building just aren't large enough to display more than a fraction of these collections. Still, it's the only museum in New York that's devoted solely to the work of Latin American and Latino artists. The art itself is invariably full of color, energy, and intensity. And, for the parent on the lookout for cultural singularity, it's a refreshing and challenging place to take the kids.

The exhibits here change with some frequency, with the exception of the Museo's *santos de palo* (saints of wood). These small devotional figures, made (between 1850 and 1940) for household use, are a uniquely Puerto Rican folk tradition. A selection from the museum's world-class collection is always on display. You'll see groupings of the Holy Family, the Trinity, the Three Kings, "lonely souls" (who are sometimes shown engulfed in flames), and assorted saints. Some of these charming pieces are crudely carved dolls; some are elegantly worked little statues, like a Saint Francis with delicate birds perching on his raised arms. A painted hand bears stigmata and, atop each finger, a member of the Holy Family. All look chipped, battered; like favorite toys, they seem well-loved and well-used. Clearly written bilingual wall panels explain the history, uses, and hidden meanings of the santos, and in one little corner you'll find a work area and activity guides in both Spanish and English. Using paper, feathers, beads, and other craft items, children are encouraged to create their own santos. For some reason, the masks provided to illustrate the concept of an icon include likenesses of John Glenn and Hillary Clinton.

Call before visiting to find out what else is on exhibit. You might see politically charged art from Chile, candid photographs of Brazilians in New York practicing Capoeira, a martial art devised by African slaves that resembles a form of dance, Mexican masks, or pre-Columbian ceremonial objects from the Taino of the Caribbean. The exhibitions are always well documented, with bilingual labels, and small enough for young attention spans. The small gift shop has Roberto Clemente T-shirts, Hispanic American Hall of Fame cards, Spanish magnetic-poetry sets, and plenty of colorful wooden toys and gimcracks, like toucan-handle letter openers and wedding dolls.

Museum of American Folk Art

Two Lincoln Square, Columbus Avenue bet. 65th and 66th Streets
212-595-9533
www.folkartmus.org
Closed: Mondays

All ages

Getting there:
1 or 9 to 66th Street

For many New Yorkers, the words "folk art" conjure up awful embroidered gingham pillows and twee mailboxes. A visit to this tranquil, modern haven across the street from Lincoln Center should clear up that misconception. *The Flag Gate,* for example, made in 1876, is a farm gate built out of wood, brass, and iron as a replica of the Stars and Stripes. It's sturdy and useful-looking, but imbued with a rippling beauty that makes it profoundly pleasing. At its best, the Americana on display here has integrity, optimism, and soul. Children will pick up that aura, not least because it's communicated through simple-seeming materials and subjects. Nothing fake, nothing phony.

Whatever temporary exhibition passes through—Amish quilts, paintings—you can usually count on seeing the most loved treasures from the museum's permanent collection. For example, the weathervanes, the most spectacular of which is a giant copper sculpture of the Native American chief Tammany, standing on an arrow and holding his bow. Among the decoys, look for ferocious little painted fishes and a beguiling black duck, asleep, that dates from 1930. Decorated notebooks are big here, and so are portraits, painted to order as we would commission a formal

photograph. But the boxes are the winners. Among these you'll want to find the sample box that belonged to a couple of nineteenth-century New Hampshire painters. Their panels of wood grain and stenciling are extraordinary. And speaking of extra-ordinary, all kinds of unusual treats are available at the gift shop, particularly at Christmastime (see page 150).

N.B. In 2001 the museum is due to open its new main building at 45-47 West 53rd Street, right next to the Museum of Modern Art. With four floors of exhibition space, self-guided discovery tours for kids, puppet shows, and craft workshops, it should be a major draw. The current gallery will stay open, a per-fect place to spend a little time if you're early for the IMAX show at the Sony theater or a performance at Lincoln Center.

Museum of Jewish Heritage

18 First Place, Battery Park City
212-509-6130
www.mjhnyc.org
Closed: Saturdays, Jewish holidays,
Thanksgiving

Ages: 8 and up

Getting there: 4 or 5 to Bowling Green; 1 or 9 to Rector Street; A, E, or C to World Trade Center

The austere ziggurat that houses the Museum of Jewish Heritage is conspicuous amid Battery Park's lush greenery. Its mission is just as distinct: to document twentieth-century Jewish experience—the Holocaust, the society it destroyed, and its aftermath. To evoke a lost world, the museum deploys artifacts, artworks, and intricate multi-media installations (including documentary footage and interviews with survivors). The bitter story told here can be understood at a simple level, yet there is more than enough on display to reward adult attention. A visit makes a fine way to teach children some painful history almost painlessly.

Each of the museum's three floors is organized around a theme. The first-floor exhibition covers Jewish life before the war. You enter a dark, high-ceilinged room hung with projection screens. Shifting images surround you: faces, candles, old pictures. You hear snatches of prayers and songs. The words and music overlap; the sense of an ancient and continuing culture comes across loud and clear. Moving through, you'll see vestiges of that culture in all its detail and diversity: a child's autograph book, a cowbell used by a New York junk peddler, a doctoral diploma from the University of Vienna. Most impressive is the Steinberger Sukkah, a cloth which was hung on the inside wall of one of the tentlike structures that observant Jews eat, pray, and occasionally live in during the harvest festival. Painted in the 20s and 30s by a Kosher slaughterer, it's covered with prayers and beautifully rendered scenes, both biblical and contemporary. On a video screen, the artist's sons reminisce about family members and local landmarks depicted on the cloth.

The grimmest part of the story is told on the second floor. There are plenty of nightmare-inducing pictures here, but you can bypass them and still give your youngsters a sense of this gruesome time. Look at the children's board game called Jews Out, a display of yellow stars from all over Europe, or film clips of book burnings and rallies. The catalog of a Berlin art exhibition called "Degenerate Music" depicts a monkeylike black man playing a saxophone and sporting a Jewish star. The most powerful sight is a group of panels covered from top to bottom with little snapshots of people. At the bottom of each column is a loose-leaf notebook with the name and fate of each person pictured. All were victims of the Holocaust.

The top floor depicts Jewish life since 1945. Inevitably, it's anticlimactic, except for the last gallery, full of windows, where there's a little cafe. Sit and look out across the water. Those ornate towers in the distance are Ellis Island; an appropriate view for the end of your tour.

Museum of Modern Art

**11 West 53rd Street bet. Fifth
and Sixth Avenues
212-708-9400**
www.moma.org.
Closed: Wednesdays

**Ages:
You decide!**

**Getting there:
E or F to Fifth
Avenue**

When you're ready to show your children the best modern art in the world, come here. And there's something about the way the place is laid out—spacious and airy, with escalators and views of the sculpture garden—that makes wandering around inside the Museum of Modern Art feel carefree and not remotely like a chore. Two suggestions: Head straight for the world-famous masterpieces—they're world-famous for a reason—and travel chronologically, which means starting at ground zero, the second floor.

Right off the bat, you have van Gogh, Gauguin, Cézanne, Seurat, and Toulouse–Lautrec. Ask the children what they think of van Gogh's *Starry Night* (probably the museum's most popular painting), and if they find it a bit strange, you can tell them the artist was a bit strange, too. Seurat's techniques are immediately appealing (all those dots!), and so are the glorious velvety textures of Rousseau's *Sleeping Gypsy* and *The Dream*. Chagall never fails, especially the fairytale-like

I and the Village, with its beautifully realized animals. Make sure to find Monet's *Water Lilies,* undulating over three walls of a room. Mondrian is pretty, Klee's just fabulous and Miro is irresistible, particularly if your children love Tove Jansson's *Moomintroll* books.

There are, of course, oodles of Picassos. Perhaps because of what we know about him now, many of his paintings of women look brutal. His early works are less disturbing—*Boy Leading a Horse,* for example, or the Cubist pieces.

The second floor must-see list also includes: Andrew Wyeth's *Christina's World,* Dubuffet's *Grand Jazz Band,* some marvelous Giacometti sculptures and two classic Hoppers, *Gas* and *House by the Railroad.*

The third floor picks up after World War II. Jasper Johns's *Flag,* and Robert Rauschenberg's mysterious collage called *First Landing Jump* (which features a Connecticut license plate, a cobalt-blue lamp, and a tire) will intrigue, and Rauschenberg's *Bed* charms with its real, though tiny, set of quilt, pillow, and sheets. Boldly lead them onward through the Surrealists (the oozy clock-faces by Dali always draw double-takes) to Claes Oldenburg's giant, squishy ice-cream cone. They'll love it all, and when you finally arrive at Rothko's huge slabs of color or Carl Andre's 144 lead squares on the floor, you can have a spirited conversation about what constitutes art (and we bet you'll end up sounding like your parents).

The icing on the cake is the top-floor design collection. Poised right above you as you take the escalator is a green Bell helicopter, with a bubble cockpit that makes it look like a dragonfly. Walk past the sleek E-type Jaguar and the architectural models and into the design galleries. By now it will seem normal to look at coffeetables, whisks, and bike locks as art objects. MoMA does that to you.

Congratulate yourselves in the spiffy Garden Cafe, where you can enjoy simple, well-prepared salads, sandwiches, and brownies while looking out at the Sculpture Garden. The gift shops (there are two, one in the building and the other across the street) are among the best museum shops in the city.

Museum of Television and Radio

25 West 52nd Street at Fifth Avenue
212-621-6600
www.mtr.org
Closed: Mondays

Ages: 5 and up

Getting there: E or F to Fifth Avenue and 53rd Street; N or R to 49th Street and Broadway; 1 or 9 to Broadway and 50th Street; B, D, F, or Q to 47th-50th Street/ Rockefeller Center

It seems fitting that the New York branch of the Museum of Television and Radio (there's one in L.A.) should be situated next to the '21' Club. Both are dedicated to guilty pleasures: '21' to luxurious dining at prices larger than some national budgets, the Museum of Television and Radio to reruns.

Call your favorite oldies "classic" if you want to justify the urge to sit placidly with your children and watch buckets of old TV shows.

Whatever you call them, the mother lode is here: more than 100,000 television and radio broadcasts—not just standbys like *The Lone Ranger, The Ed Sullivan Show* (hey,

wanna see the Beatles' first appearance?) and *I Love Lucy,* but *Philco Playhouse, Sgt. Bilko,* and lots more. (Some archival items must be requested in advance). You can call up as many as four selections on the computer and then watch them on a console for up to two hours.

C hildren accustomed to passing family trips with books on tape can be persuaded to listen to old radio shows; the Orson Welles *War of the Worlds* is still a grabber (and so is the story that goes with it). All of this is in addition to the regular programs that go on in various screening rooms throughout the day. Offerings range from programs of old commercials to Hitchcock retrospectives to broader themes (such as Elvis on TV or a *Ben Stiller Show* retrospective). Pick up a schedule of the day's selection on your way in, and make a note of the special events for children. We like the idea of the Saturday-morning workshops called "Re-Creating Radio," when children 9 and older can produce classic serials like *Superman* or *The Shadow,* acting the parts, cuing up sound effects and music. You get to take home a cassette of your show, too. Cool.

T he small gift shop stocks a remarkable quantity of videos, books, and posters in its tiny space. Here's the place to fill in the holes in your Bob-and-Ray audiotape collection.

M useum of the City of New York

1220 Fifth Avenue at 103rd Street
212-534-1672
www.mcny.org
Closed: Mondays

All ages

Getting there:
6 to 103rd
Street

J ust like any old-time town museum, this one tells its story through cutlery and chinaware, maps and firefighting equipment, portraits and furniture. This might be compelling to you, but when children are involved, cut to the chase. Start on the top (fifth) floor, and get the kids to imagine that the two nineteenth-century rooms from the Fifth Avenue home of John D. Rockefeller belong to them. The palatial master bedroom will knock your collective socks off, with its exotic mélange of styles—Turkish, Moorish, Anglo-Japanese—and its sleigh bed, colored-glass detail, and inlaid everything. It's hard to know where you'd stow your toys.

S peaking of which, two floors down are the antique dollhouses, the jewels of the museum's collection. To reach them

91

you'll pass through a small exhibit of antique play-things, from rusty roller skates to tin soldiers. While children love toys, they don't love other people's, especially if they're rusty, so don't expect much interest. But the 12 houses, ranging in date from 1767 to 1998, with their tiny lights gleaming in the dim gallery, are breathtaking. Sit on one of the stools scattered about; take your time.

Of our two favorites, the Briggs Dream House provides a delightful contrast to all the dainty sprigged wallpaper and elaborate table settings you'll see in the others. Mr Briggs worked at the museum for years and during that time he built a model of the home he would have liked: circa 1930, it's white clapboard on the outside and on the inside, utterly masculine, with an artist's studio and workroom in the attic, an Art Deco bedroom, ashtrays, fabulous tiny phones, nautical prints, a cannon, and a jar on the mantelpiece containing (we're told) six grains of tobacco. Across from it, utterly contemporary and utterly mysterious, is the Cultural Center with a Mysterious Locked Room, done in "the confused style." In a fantastical dwelling with overtones of T*he Nightmare Before Christmas,* dancers swirl, birds and giant insects preside, and people stand on the "pastry terrace" (!) with, yes, pastries.

One floor down, the exhibition called "Port of the New World" has a gigantic statue of Robert Fulton (of Ferry fame), figureheads and some excellent dioramas: a bustling South

Street, Verrazzano confronting some scantily clad Native Americans on Staten Island, and Henry Hudson on the *Half Moon* (which, incidentally, was only 63 feet long). There are some lovely ship models here, too, which will afford you all the opportunity to brush up on the differences between sloop, brig, and frigate.

If it's been a success this far, you could try them on the maps and cutlery, but don't say we didn't warn you. The gift shop is full of books, posters, T-shirts, and toys that lean toward the classic (spaldeens, yo-yos, toy theaters).

National Museum of the American Indian

Smithsonian Institution, 1 Bowling Green
212-668-6624
www.si.edu/nmai
Closed: Christmas Day

Ages: 5 and up

Getting there: 4 or 5 to Bowling Green; 1 or 9 to South Ferry; N or R to Whitehall Street

A unique museum in a spectacular setting, this collection is best appreciated by older children who already know something about the native peoples of the Americas and have a real interest in them. Not that young kids will be bored. Throughout the galleries, they'll find drawers to open, which contain such treasures as Pan pipes, toy lacrosse sticks, pieces of fur, and woven fabrics to play with. They'll have fun, but the real mission of the N.M.AI. is too esoteric for them.

Instead of illustrating an objectified historical record of battles and tribes, this museum aims to convey the experience of being an American Indian by showing the domestic and ceremonial objects of Indian life, accompanied by the commentary of living Indians. You don't just look at a kayak and the elaborately fashioned, hooded anorak that a fisherman wore; you listen to an actual fisherman's recorded voice talking about these tools and how they were made and used. Similarly, you have to read the accompanying texts to learn why the little dolls and models on display are more than playthings.

The exhibition rooms are organized around broad themes—creation myths, domestic life—rather than individual tribes or time periods. The objects are breathtaking—particularly the masks, the 1,800-year-old duck decoys, the beautifully woven hats, and the jewelry made of beads, quills, and feathers. The sight that will stay with you long after you've left is the Moccasin Round Dance: dozens of pairs of Indian moccasins of all shapes and sizes set in a great circle, the left foot of each pair raised as if in a dance. A wedge in the circular display case is missing, so visitors can enter and complete the round.

The Resource Center, across the hall from the gallery entrance, contains reading material, objects to handle, and computer stations equipped with interactive programs on different aspects of Indian life and history. On one, you can learn a bit of the Lenape language; at another, you can play a drum that appears on the monitor by tapping the screen. Many of the staff here are Native Americans (one is a descendant of Sitting Bull), and they're eager to share their knowledge.

Before you leave, be sure to take a good look at the building itself, a Beaux Arts jewel by Cass Gilbert. Check out the swooping staircase and generous use of marble. Above all (literally), don't miss the superb, W. P.A.-era ceiling murals by Reginald Marsh in the Rotunda. Skip the gallery shop on the second floor (beautiful stuff; pricey) and then take the elevator down to the museum shop (see page 151).

New York City Fire Museum

278 Spring Street bet. Hudson
and Varick Streets
212-691-1303
http.nyfd.com/museum.html
Closed: Mondays

All ages

Getting there:
1 or 9 to
Houston
Street; C or E
to Spring
Street

After a visit to this Beaux Arts SoHo firehouse, with its antique fire engines and elaborate displays, your children will certainly remember one thing: the stuffed dog. Forget Balto. This remarkable mutt ambled into a Brooklyn firehouse in 1929 and found his vocation—climbing ladders, sliding down the pole, riding on the fire engines, and, most significantly, dashing into buildings to search for victims, even extending himself for cats and kittens. In the line of duty he was scalded, cut, bruised, and run over twice. A hit-and-run driver ended the dog's life in 1938, and his inconsolable pals had him stuffed and put on display. Now he sits regally in a glass case with a medal pinned onto his red throne, inscribed, "Kindness The Poetry of the Soul" (sic).

Hard to top that exhibit, but there is more excellent stuff here. The high-ceilinged ground floor houses painted leather buckets from the Victorian era (each household was required to have two) and gorgeous, gleaming antique fire engines, resplendent with gauges, levers, lanterns, and stirring names (Tiger, Metropolitan Steamer). One snub-nosed beauty has eight enormous searchlights on top. Children are not allowed to climb on the engines; alas, there is no real fire engine here to clamber in—not yet, anyway. They can pose on the running boards for a photo. Give the very large, very loud bell a ring, and ask a guard to sound the exciting wind-up alarm on one of the engines. And all the while, you can monitor the steady to-and-fro of the dispatchers keeping in touch with firefighting units all over New York. If there's a brush fire on Staten Island or a conflagration in a Manhattan high-rise, you'll hear about it as it happens.

Around the walls are lots of photographs and displays concerning fire-fighting history (hydrants, bell towers, reservoirs, alarms), many of them quite esoteric. Look for the photographs of horses thundering full tilt toward fires. Apparently these animals were so well trained that when the alarm sounded they would immediately line up by their own rigs. The tools, mostly axes, are scary and impressive, as are the Jaws of Life, wedged into a burnt-out section of a car's chassis. The firemen's pole is in a back corner. At the other corner, there's a small annex containing many jolly snapshots of New York City firehouses and their smiling personnel, as well as badges from fire companies around the world.

Upstairs you'll find metal fire marks, lots of them. You may be interested to know that these marks were created for insurance purposes; your children won't. But they'll be (briefly) intrigued by the wonderful tin models and ornate nineteenth-century engines sporting plumes, big painted wheels, and lanterns with colored, etched glass.

This small place has a unique feel. To be really cool, why not tell your child's teacher that school groups get to crawl out of a smoke-filled room as part of an exercise in fire safety? And if you see a group of kids taking a tour while you're there, it's worth tagging along on the off chance you'll get to join them. On the way out, dawdle at the excellent gift shop (see page 151).

New York City Police Museum

25 Broadway at Beaver Street
212-301-4440
www.nycpolicemuseum.org
Open: daily

Ages: 6 and up

Getting there:
4 or 5 to
Bowling
Green

The Police Museum is one of the city's relatively unknown gems, which is surprising considering that it's been around since 1929 and contains the world's largest collection of police apparatus and memorabilia, much of it fascinating to kids. Now moved from its somewhat dingy former home on the second floor of the Police Academy to spacious new quarters in the Bowling Green post office, it's likely to be discovered.

Some of the artifacts here date back a hundred years. There are handcuffs, helmets, Al Capone's terrifying tommy gun, and an array of modern-era vehicles——a cruiser, a scooter, a motorcycle——that you can get into or onto. You can trace the history of nightstick design, learn how to spot a counterfeit bill, or stand in a lineup next to a life-size caricature of Capone (who looks surprisingly short). You can take your own fingerprints and look at enlargements of Pretty

Boy Floyd's after he'd tried to obliterate them with acid. Kids who like to draw will be fascinated by the forensic-art display, which shows how police artists work up sketches of suspects based on the verbal descriptions of witnesses. And everyone will be impressed by the lurid black-and-white photos of old-time mobsters (some after having been rubbed out!), the sawed-off shotgun in the violin case, and the grim array of weapons confiscated from juveniles: zip guns, machetes, a screw-studded baseball bat.

The big news in this new venue is the firearm simulator, a screen-projection device used in police training. Participants carry a gun and a can of pepper spray (the innards of both have been replaced with lasers) and face a screen that shows various scenarios from the cop's point of view. It's as absorbing and addictive as any shoot-'em-up game, so it's a real pity that you have to be 18 to play. Fortunately, you can assuage the feelings of disappointed kids with an authentic (and *really* loud) police whistle or an NYPD baseball cap from the small but inviting gift shop downstairs.

While you're there, don't forget to look at the main hall of the post office. This was once the Cunard Building, where travelers booked passages on ships like the *Lusitania* and, yes, even the *Titanic* (that should grab the kids' interest). From the museum, which is on the second floor, there are some wonderful views of the ornate vaulted ceiling and its grandiose murals. They really don't build 'em like they used to.

New York Hall of Science

47-01 111th Street, at Flushing Meadows, Corona Park, Queens
718-699-0005
www.nyhallsci.org
Closed: Labor Day, Thanksgiving, Christmas Eve, Christmas Day, and New Year's Day

All ages

Getting there: 7 to Willets Point/Shea Stadium

The New York Hall of Science, like the Queens Museum and the Unisphere, is a splendid relic of the world's fair: a quirky building in the shape of an undulating curtain with a round, high-ceilinged entry hall. A welcome antidote to those who find the Liberty Science Center a little too show-biz, the Hall of Science is not flashy, noisy, or packed (normally). And the friendly, well-informed young staffers are eager and able to pull a shy youngster into the swim.

This is an interactive museum par excellence, with umpteen scientific tricks up its sleeve. Older kids will learn from what they're doing; the little ones

will be having so much fun they won't realize it's educational. What kid can resist a giant bubble maker or a 400-pound pendulum whose swing you can change by throwing magnets at it? Or a windmill whose direction is altered by swiveling banks of massed fans? "Singing Shadows" is a room that transforms your every movement into sound "Recollections," a backlit screen that colors, distorts, and reflects the movement of the people who cluster in front of it. Twice daily there's a dissection of a cow's eye.

On the upper floor, get a closer look at the Rotosphere, the huge, clockworklike sculpture that slowly, perpetually rotates in the rotunda. Now study the circular balustrade you're leaning on. See those thick glass lenses embedded in it? Under them are pictures, each taken exactly 10 kilometers from the Hall of Science, at five-degree intervals around the full 360 degrees. Up here is the entrance to the science playground, the world's second-largest (after Bombay's). It's worth the extra fee. This colorful, inviting place really does translate scientific principles into physical fun. To explain Newton's Third Law ("For every action there's an equal and opposite reaction"), kids climb on a flexible, steel-reinforced rope web that resembles a jungle gym with bounce. A giant seesaw demonstrates leverage, and, by turning an Archimedes screw, kids make water flow uphill, then cascade down. Best of all during the summer dog days is the Kinetic Sculpture; the gentle spray of water coming from the top is called a fog machine, and it'll leave you feeling 10 degrees cooler.

The spacious dining area offers only vending-machine snacks, but has an intriguing device that, for 51 cents, will squash your penny before your very eyes and return it as a thin oval bearing a caricature of Albert Einstein. The perfect souvenir! Don't skip the gift shop, though (see page 152); it's packed with both serious and goofy stuff. And on your way out, drop some change into the big, black Vortex and watch the coins accelerate up to 60 miles per hour before disappearing down the hole. Go crazy, drop in some more change; it's a donation.

New York Transit Museum

Schermerhorn Street and Boerum Place, Brooklyn Heights, Brooklyn
718-243-3060
www.mta.nyc.ny.us/museum/general.htm
Closed: Mondays

All ages

Getting there:
2, 3, 4, or 5 to
Borough Hall

Perfectly situated in a defunct subway station, this is just the place in which to celebrate the glories of the world's biggest and most complicated rapid-transit system. Since these glories include 722 miles of track, 463 station stops, a fare that has increased 30-fold, and a history that spans the century, the Transit Museum is a densely packed repository, much of which—like the massed turnstiles and scale models—will intrigue the children, while the old subway maps, vintage photos, and Miss Subways tchotchkes will carry Proustian echoes for parents. You and your family can spend a happy hour or two and emerge knowing quite a bit about the subway. And it's cool down there, too, even in high summer.

Begin your visit one flight down and past the token kiosk at "Stone, Steel and Backbone," a text-and-pictures exhibition that gives an overview of the subway's construction. There's a lot here, and the big blocks of text on the walls can be daunting even for the adult non-train-buff, but it's broken up with enough artifacts (a surveyor's chain, a detonator) and tales of disaster (like the 1903 Washington Heights explosion, whose 10 victims were reported as "Timothy Sullivan, William Shuette, and eight unidentified Italians") that it's worth a quick trip through, for scene-setting purposes. As your kids drag you past the display of subway orna-mentation, check out the photos of the splendid (but closed) City Hall station. All the way back on the first floor are some vintage buses, superb scale models, and one of the museum's most popular attractions: a

bus cab. Kids love to climb in and play driver, steering through pretend killer midtown traffic.

Down one more flight, at track level, is the best part: beautifully restored vintage cars, lined up as if ready to pull out. Students of subway strap design will note a clear deterioration over the years; parents of a certain age may feel compelled to share memories of the straw-seated cars with bare light bulbs and chunky overhead fans of the type featured so heavily in films of the 40s. Children will just want to race in and out of the cars, and that's allowed. Don't forget to admire Money Car "G," New York City's oldest extant rapid-transit car, an elegant little carriage that was in continuous service for 77 years.

The Transit Museum holds frequent Saturday workshops in which kids can do things like build a model of the Brooklyn Bridge or make paper station mosaics. Visit the gift shop, where you'll find one mysterious item: Amid the books for buffs, quaint rubber stamps, Y-cut-token jewelry and Thomas the Tank Engine stuff, the New York City Transit Museum sells glitter makeup.

New York Unearthed

17 State Street near Whitehall Street
212-748-8628
www.southstseaport.org
Closed: Weekends

Ages: 8 and up

Getting there:
1 or 9 to South
Ferry; 4 or 5
to Bowling
Green; N or R
to Whitehall
Street

Tucked away between the bustle of Wall Street and the great downtown tourist hub (Battery Park and the boats for Ellis Island, Staten Island, and the Statue of Liberty), you'll find a quiet, cobblestone court-yard with trees. Just inside is New York Unearthed, a tiny place that's home to 10 small display cases, each one containing a diorama and a handful of objects found in the area (mostly) and illustrating a phase of New York history, from Native American arrow-heads 6,000 years old to the debris of a 1950s diner. There are clay pipes from the Dutch era, marbles, wine jugs, and more clay pipes from a British tavern, pieces of pre-cious stone from a silver-smith's shop of the 1790s, and so on. The cases are beautifully designed and laid out, the

wording is perfectly clear and not too overwhelming. Look for the nineteenth-century porcelain "Frozen Charlotte" dolls; tiny and white, with immovable limbs, they were named after a little girl who froze to death in a popular children's story of the day. There's a toy tea set, too.

The big excitement is downstairs, where, inside a glass-walled conservation lab, an actual, living archaeologist sits, busying himself/herself with animal bones, old glass bottles, and shards of pottery. The archaeologists are very friendly. "We tend to come out," said one, cheerfully, "and very often we invite children into the lab." Inside, you can handle the bones and ceramics and, if you're lucky, dip a "conductivity meter" into little yogurt pots in which artifacts are being soaked to have the salt crystals acquired over the centuries leached away. The archaeologist will explain the significance of everything you see, including the yellow cabinet with the word "ACID" written on it in large red letters. On the wall facing the lab is an ingenious mock-up of an archaeological cross-section, with objects lying in seven strata. It even includes a modern-day site, with soda bottle and Batman cup, to remind us that these are the treasures of the future. And speaking of the future, one day the Disneyish "elevator" might be working. An unlikely component of this sweetly scholarly place, it apparently gives the illusion of moving down into the bowels of a dig, enhanced with sound-and-light effects. You'll be the judge of that.

N Isamu Noguchi Garden Museum

32-37 Vernon Boulevard, Long Island City, Queens
718-721-1932
www.noguchi.org
Closed: Mondays, Tuesdays;
also November through March

Ages: 5 and up

Getting there: By bus, shuttle from the Asia Society (725 Park Avenue) on weekends (call 718-204-7088 for details). By subway, N to Broadway in Queens, walk west (see below). By tram, Roosevelt Island tram from Manhattan, free bus to the bridge, then walk.

Follow the example of visitors from all over the world and make the (shorter than you imagine) pilgrimage to Long Island City to visit this extraordinary museum of Isamu Noguchi's sculpture. If you're going by subway, take the N train to Broadway and walk west toward Vernon Boulevard and the East River. The dense commercial traffic gives way to residential streets and then warehouses. At Vernon, turn left and walk a block to 33rd Road. Look carefully up 33rd, and you will see that the nondescript gray building that faces Vernon isn't so nondescript after all.

Almost 40 years ago Noguchi established his studio on Vernon Boulevard in order to be close to the marble suppliers operating in the vicinity. In 1975 he turned this building, former-ly a photoengraving plant, into a museum for his work, adding to it while being careful not to disrupt its continuity with its surroundings. The result is probably the most hidden-away museum in the city, as well as the most profoundly serene.

Here you'll find more than 250 works in stone, metal, wood, paper, and clay, carefully arranged by the artist himself in 13 galleries and a garden. Monumental, spare, and abstract, they're immediately attractive to children, particularly if you can explain what Noguchi had in mind while he was creating them. The informative free handout will help. It says that Noguchi was preoccupied with opposites—smooth and rough, together but separate, hollow and filled, and so on— that to him represented the human condition, much as he felt stone did, with its irregular shapes and

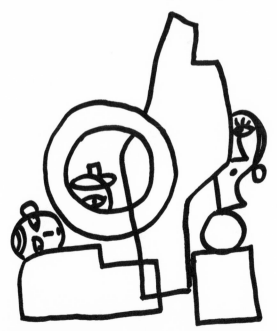

great capacity to endure. (We know you can find a way to communicate this!)

The best examples of this high-but-simple-concept are the powerful, imposing stone and metal pieces in the ground-floor galleries. In the garden, kids will adore Noguchi's take on the traditional Japanese fountain, the *tsukubai,* a massive stone cube from, and over, which water flows so quietly and smoothly that the stone seems sheathed in glass.

Don't miss the upper floor, where everything is on a smaller scale and the feel is more playful. Here you'll find Noguchi's famous cocoonlike paper lampshades (known as Akari light sculptures), gorgeous, sinuous bronzes, and meticulously detailed architectural models for plazas, stage sets, slides, and fountains. You, the parents, will get a big kick out of the Guardian Ear and Radio Nurse—a tactile, rounded baby monitor made out of Bakelite and metal in the 30s. Speaking of tactile, don't touch a thing, however much you may want to. As any guide will explain, the natural oils in human hands damage the stone. Tell the children not to fret; a very different, very hands-on museum is just a short walk away (see Socrates Sculpture Park).

N.B. Enthusiasts can stay to watch video documentaries on Noguchi in the first-floor video room.

Old Stone House Historic Interpretive Center

J. J. Byrne Park, Third Street bet. Fourth and Fifth Avenues, Park Slope, Brooklyn
718-768-3195
Open: Saturday afternoons

All ages

Getting there: F G, M, or N to Ninth Street and Fourth Avenue

This pretty little stone house, sitting in the middle of a Park Slope playground, has been at the heart of Brooklyn life for 300 years. Originally a Dutch farmhouse, built in 1699, it was the site of a bloody action at the Battle of Brooklyn—the first, and largest, battle of the War for Independence. Later it was a clubhouse for the Brooklyns, the baseball team that became the Dodgers. Walt Whitman called the building Old Iron Nines, referring to the metal numbers embedded in its north-facing wall that mark the year it was built.

Over the years the structure was partially buried, then fell into disrepair until it was rediscovered in 1933 by a W. P.A. archaeological team. Now, splendidly rebuilt and restored with the original stone a few feet from its first site, it's open for business on Saturdays with a small permanent exhibition and all sorts of special events: storytelling, lectures, concerts and historical re-enactments. For the young history buff, it offers a chance to explore the past in a microcosm; quite a bit is known about what happened in this one particular place—and with good reason.

The permanent exhibition features pictures of the house at various points in its long life, looking more or less the same as its surroundings change from deeply pastoral to throughly urban. But most of the material here is about the house's role in the Battle of Brooklyn. It was here that General William Hamilton (Lord Stirling) led some 400 Marylanders against a force of British and Hessians numbering around 2,000. After repeated assaults, the decimated Marylanders captured the house briefly, only to be overwhelmed and taken prisoner. But Hamilton's diversionary action worked, enabling the main body of the American army to escape and fight another day. By the way, the school across the street is named after Hamilton.

The drama of the fighting is captured superbly in the exhibition's centerpiece, a highly detailed scale model of the Old Stone House during the battle, with tiny soldiers, horses, and a cannon belching great plumes of (cotton) smoke. A kid can spend serious time examining this model; the accompanying text is as detailed as the model itself, so you can follow the course of battle very closely. The tiny troops are in precisely accurate uniforms and carry just the right weapons; their minute faces grimace and frown, listen and shout.

In its upstairs hall, the Old Stone House offers year-round concerts, storytelling, and lectures for both children and adults. This small, unassuming landmark packs a lot of history into a very small space—and right outside the door is a very spiffy playground.

Queens Museum of Art and Panorama of the City of New York

Flushing Meadows, Corona Park, Queens
718-592-9700
www.queensmuse.org
Closed: Mondays;
open Tuesdays to groups by appointment

All ages

Getting there: 7 from Times Square to Willets Point/Shea Stadium

Flushing Meadows in Queens has many delights, ideally explored without the hassle of a car. Part of the fun is stepping off the Number 7 train into the spacious, grassy park that is the place where two celebrated world's fairs were held. Checking on their remains offers adults

113

an archaeological *frisson,* and the scale of the surviving structures will make the kids giddy and exultant.

Most of the galleries at the Queens Museum are given over to temporary exhibitions, but you'll also find one of New York's most fascinating family attractions: the Panorama of the City of New York, which is an architectural scale model of the city, all five boroughs of it. The Panorama currently contains 895,000 tiny buildings, as well as highways, bridges and other landmarks, and you can walk around the edge of the whole area on a glass-bottomed ramp built a few feet above it. The large room is subdued; rapt people point and peer, looking for their particular landmarks. At regu-

lar intervals the sky darkens to night, little lights gleam from within some of the houses, and a tiny plane on a wire takes off from La Guardia! It's a heady experience, especially for kids, who get to feel big in New York City. By the way, bring binoculars to focus in on your own building.

Also on permanent—or at least very long-lived—display at the museum are its collections of Tiffany glass and world's fair memorabilia. Either is capable of holding a young attention span for, oh, maybe 10 minutes——as is the gift shop, though the prices on the authentic world's fair objects will make the whole family blink. But why bother with, say, a picture of the Unisphere when the real thing is right outside?

If you've only seen it through traffic on the accursed L.I.E., prepare to be amazed. It is, after all, the largest globe in the world. Made for the 1964 fair, the spherical grid with steel plates for continents is 140 feet high and weighs 700,000 pounds. In the summer, fountains play around it. When the water's off, skaters tear around the empty basin, dodging the pipes and floodlights and passing cops. (It's hard to resist. Still, no-one's supposed to be in there). The paths around the sphere, however, are flat and smooth, ideal for both skating and boarding. Bring the camera.

R Theodore oosevelt Birthplace

**28 East 20th Street bet. Park Avenue
and Broadway**
212-260-1616
www.nps.gov
Closed: Mondays, Tuesdays

Ages: 8 and up

Getting there:
4, 5, 6, L, N,
or R to Union
Square/14th
Street, N or R
to 23rd Street

Historic houses are not high on any kid's list of places to see, but this one could be an exception, particularly if you prepare your child by saying that this was the home of a frail, sheltered boy who grew up to be a rugged hero and the only New Yorker ever elected President. Then there's the teddy-bear thing. Teddy bears are named after Theodore Roosevelt; you can get the story and inspect some of the world's very first specimens in the garden-floor museum while waiting for your tour to begin. (You need to take the tour in order to see the restored rooms on the upper floors). The museum has some good stuff: toys (including a doll's tea-set of startling delicacy), a moose head shot by T. R. himself, and T. R.'s well-worn Rough Rider uniform and gear. Plop yourself down in front of the monitor and watch a segment from the A&E "Biography" series that's playing. With luck you'll catch the wonderful bit about the charge up San Juan Hill and not the story behind T. R.'s abortive gubernatorial campaign, which could douse anyone's interest.

The tour is short, 30 minutes or so, and the guides know how to pepper the history with oddball factoids, which keep kids absorbed. They know, for instance, what the bulbous, gloomily upholstered chairs in the library are stuffed with—horsehair, since you ask; and why they're bunched in the middle of the room—because the only source of gas for light was the central chandelier. That rubber wire running from it to the little, porcelain-shaded lamp is an extension cord. The windows in the nursery lead out onto a gymnasium that T. R.'s father added onto the house so that the children could exercise regularly. This is where T. R. began the pursuit of "the strenuous life" that turned a sickly, asthmatic kid into a big-game-hunting, Amazon-exploring, rough-riding military hero, a president who could declare, "I feel like a bull moose!" and mean it.

Today's asthmatic children may be amazed to learn that the therapies inflicted on young Theodore included inhaling cigar smoke and drinking black coffee. All kids will be amused to learn that indoor plumbing in these days was only for the very wealthy.

A second museum on the parlor floor contains a stuffed lion and a couple of birds prepared by the young T. R. himself, along with assorted heads, antlers, and photos of the great man with huge dead fish. If your environmentally sensitive little ones are disturbed by these brazen trophies, steer them to the display which details T. R.'s pioneering contributions as a conservationist. It's just to the left of the lion. Oh, and the modest gift shop has a nice selection of—what else?—teddy bears.

Rose Center for Earth and Space

Central Park West at 81st Street
Open: The year 2000

Ages: 6 and up

Getting there:
1 or 9 to 79th
Street; B or C
to 81st Street

Yes, the planetarium is at long last due to reopen, so it naturally deserves a place in this book. One piece of this elaborate facility, the Gottesman Hall of Planet Earth, is already up and running, just off the Hall of

Biodiversity. The focus here is geology, and you can look at an ice-core sample from Greenland that shows how the climate changed thousands of years ago, impressive samples of undersea volcanic chimneys ("black smokers"), and a huge slice of quarried rock.

That's all fine, but we're waiting for the wonderful dome that's slowly taking shape behind the parking lot. What was so great about the old planetarium was its virtual-reality aspect, the way it conjured up the illusion of a starry sky. Virtual reality has come a long way recently. Here's what to expect. In the top half of the new sphere, the Space Theater will use the most advanced technology (a specially-made, one-of-a-kind Zeiss projector) to depict the wonders of the universe; a laser system will provide "full-dome coverage" and the 9,100 stars displayed will twinkle. In the lower half of the dome, the Big Bang Theater will bring you-are-there immediacy to nothing less than the creation of the universe. From there, visitors will walk the Cosmic Pathway (!), a spiraling ramp that apparently demonstrates 13

billion years of evolution (at 3 million years per inch), ending up in the Hall of the Universe, where you can all fall upon interactive gizmos that will, presumably, explain astrophysics and other impenetrable subjects.

This sounds very fancy indeed. No word yet as to whether the planetarium will resume its nighttime laser shows accompanied by the music of Pink Floyd—a perennial favorite with teenagers. No word either as to whether the Space Theater will have the much-loved New York skyline silhouette along the lower edge of the dome. We're hoping.

Socrates Sculpture Park

Broadway at Vernon Boulevard,
Long Island City, Queens
718-956-1819
www.queens.nyc.ny.us/places/socrates.html
Open: Daily

All ages

Getting there:
N to
Broadway,
then Q103 or
Q104 bus

Strewn with contemporary sculpture and set against striking views of the East River, Roosevelt Island, and the Upper East Side, Socrates Sculpture Park is probably the city's most unusual picnic spot, as well as its most dramatic venue for large-scale, outdoor art. Formerly an illegal dump-site, it's the brainchild of sculptor Mark di Suvero, who, in the 80s, got the city to take over the four-and-a-half-acre lot and lease it back to his group for a dollar a year. They cleared the land, which took a year, and opened the park in 1986 as an informal gallery and outdoor studio for local artists. There is one show in late spring, another in early fall. Twenty or so featured artists a year are selected through an application process. They are free to work in any medium, as long as it can stand up to the weather—and the kids.

W hich brings us to Socrates Park's most distinctive feature: Almost nothing is off-limits to children. Use your common sense, and if a piece looks receptive, go ahead—climb, touch, sit on, ride, or run around it. Many of the works seem designed for hands-on use, which makes a pleasant change from the restraint required at other places, such as

the nearby Noguchi Museum (see page 108). Since much of the art on display at Socrates is created on-site, children and their minders can get a look at working artists, too. Visit in the month or two preceding one of the semiannual shows, when artists laying bricks, grouting tiles, and stacking steel drums nearly outnumber the visitors. Even on a quiet, chilly weekend afternoon, Socrates Park is a happening place.

Since the exhibitions change, there are always surprises, but some works seem to be on permanent display: a pair of hyper-realistic statues of black teenagers and *On Fertile Ground,* an imposing (10-foot-high) wood carving of a snake clasping an egg in its jaws. Elaine Lorenz's *Gathering* has also been there for a while. True to its name, this arrangement of three curving, interwoven concrete planters draws kids of all ages to play hide and seek around it. They'll also gravitate toward *Sound Observatory,* an arrangement of metal plinths, pylons, and cylinders that are meant to be tapped, pounded, or jumped on, all assembled in front of a large metal disk that faces the East River, amplifying the percussive sound.

At first sight the park has an urban, rough-hewn look, but then you'll notice carefully arranged floral borders, and stone walls incorporating alphabet blocks. Amble toward the painted rocks at water's edge, peer around the heavy-equipment sheds, and you'll see sculptural requisites—beams, rebar, chicken wire, unfinished and inexplicable structures—laid out in an order that must be intelligible to someone. Socrates Park is always a work in progress.

South Street Seaport Museum

207 Front Street near South Street
212-748-8600
www.southstseaport.org
Open: Daily

All ages

Getting there:
2, 3, 4, 5, J, Z,
or M to Fulton
Street; A or C
to Broadway-
Nassau

For many of us, the South Street Seaport represents a dismal shopping mall for tourists and a haven for Wall Streeters getting snockered after their daily labors—but there's so much more. For a start, the place smells strongly of fish, reminding you of its reason for being. There are street entertainers and daredevil teenagers on skateboards. And the museums, both the galleries and the majestic ships, are truly evocative of the port's nineteenth-century heyday.

One ticket, purchased on the pier, will get you into everything. Start out with the museum, but be selective. Downstairs, peer

at model ships and the old bird's-eye-view maps of the harbor, including a marvelously detailed Currier and Ives. (How did the artists

see from so high, when there were no helicopters?) You can make out Coney Island, myriad churches, houses, little ships. Upstairs there's some beautiful scrimshaw and a "cutaway ship's model" of the *Queen of Bermuda* cruise ship, made in the 40s, with a cross-section painting à la David Macaulay on one side (look for the naked man in the shower, horses in the stalls, and flamenco dancers practicing). Don't miss the small section on smuggling, which shows the X-ray of the intestine of a man who has swallowed narcotics-filled condoms (you could call 'em balloons...) and a photo of a man caught with a lump of raw opium the size of a guinea pig under his hat. (The children's museum has closed, by the way, for a major rethinking and renovation.)

Next, stretch your legs on the ships. The lordly *Peking* (1911) has four masts and a below-deck where you can decode the nineteenth-century class system: best digs for the captain, second-best for the first and second mates, crummy for everyone else. Down here you can also watch a thrilling 1929 movie clip that shows this actual ship lurching through a Cape Horn storm. Across the pier sits the sturdy *Ambrose* lightship (1908), which for many years watched over the entrance to New York Harbor. The *Ambrose* is wonderful; it's small, so it moves with the water. More modern and more furnished than the other ships here, it conveys the sense that the men have just gone ashore, leaving behind their boots and soap dishes. The bridge still has its antiquated radio equipment. Parents may be intrigued by the photos of Captain Gustave Lang, who seems to have spent 29 years on board, visiting his wife and children in Queens only "briefly at the beginning of each month."

Walk down the boardwalk in the direction of Pier 17, and look to your left. You're under the bowsprits of the *Peking* and the *Wavertree* (built in 1885 and the largest iron sailing ship afloat). Imagine ten or twenty more of these stately beauties tied up here, and you'll have some idea of how it used to be in the age of sail. Finally, you all deserve a short cruise around the harbor on the historic schooner, *Pioneer.* The smiling crew may even let the children help with the sails.

Staten Island Children's Museum

Snug Harbor Cultural Center
1000 Richmond Terrace, Staten Island
718-273-2060
www.kidsmuseum.com
Closed: Mondays

Ages: Up to 8

Getting there:
S40 from
Staten Island
Ferry to Snug
Harbor

Big sculptures dot the lawn in front of the S. I. C.M.; the giant wooden grasshopper in the hard hat (there's a major expansion under way) is particularly excellent for climbing. Inside is the kid-friendliest place imaginable: small, hands-on, colorful, and aimed squarely at youthful interests and attention spans.

Spread over four floors are installations, interactive displays, puzzles, activities, and toys grouped around broad themes. The kids will love putting on aprons and sloshing around in Wonder Water, a water-play area full of sinks piled high with water wheels, pails, cups, and bottles. The most intense action is at the Babbling Brook, an area designated just for the under-5s.

The exhibitions here aren't nearly so lavish or complicated as those at better-endowed institutions, but they are clear and vibrant. In "Bugs and Other Insects," for example, a suit of armor painted bright turquoise is all that's needed to convey the idea of an exoskeleton; nearby, there's a human-size ant's chamber that kids can crawl around in. "Bridges" offers an adorably weathered model that illustrates the three different types of bridges connecting Staten Island to the rest of the world; next to it, kids can climb into pedal cars and negotiate the S.I.C.M. thruway, lumbering through three model bridges, navigating their way past a toll booth and traffic lights.

When science starts to pall, drop by Portia's Playhouse on the main floor, set up for improvised theatrics; it has costumes, a stage with a curtain to draw, light and sound boards, even a makeup table (you have to bring your own makeup). One floor down is food (a couple of vending machines) and Block Harbor, a large rec room on several levels, fixed up to resemble a ship's deck and galley. It has a reading area, a dress-up table, and zillions and zillions of blocks. The kids can play here, you can sip a soda outside, and you can all chill. If the smallest members have any energy left, explore Snug Harbor's 80 rolling acres, dotted with duck ponds and stately gardens. They might be impressed to know that the whole place was built by a reformed pirate. On a damp winter's day they might even sense the ghosts of the old salts who used to live there.

Statue of Liberty National Monument

Liberty Island (New York Harbor)
212-363-7620
www.nps.org
Closed: Christmas Day

Ages: 6 and up

Getting there:
1 or 9 to South Ferry; 4 or 5 to Bowling Green; ferry to Liberty Island (buy tickets at Castle Clinton)

You have to see it. In fact, we think you have to climb up to the crown. So, pick a year when the kids are old enough to wait in line and climb 354 vertiginous steps. Then pick your time. Carefully. The Statue of Liberty is America's most visited landmark. On any given summer day, 25,000 or so people file in through two doors. If you arrive on the first or second boat, you'll be fine. Get there later, and you may have to wait in line for a couple hours *just to get inside.* The best day to visit? According to the Park Rangers, it's Christmas Eve, when the volume of visitors is reduced by 75 percent. Failing that, aim for a weekday morning in January or February. The statue looks gorgeous whatever the weather.

Your arrival by boat is an awesome experience, particularly when you notice the emotion on the faces of other visitors, who come from every country in the world and every state in the union. You'll have the opportunity to perform a useful public service by correcting all the people who think the Verrazano-Narrows Bridge is the Brooklyn Bridge. The island itself is smaller than you expect, with gulls and helicopters wheeling, kids scampering on the grass, and lower Manhattan spread out before you. No loitering yet, though; you have serious business.

If you're accompanied by little children or fragile tourists, you should know that the observation deck offers a breathtaking view and is easily reachable by elevator. If you're going for the crown, take a bottle of water. The temperature is 20 higher warmer than outside, and the atmosphere gets claustrophobic as you wind your way up between the Statue's iron skeleton, brilliantly designed by Gustave Eiffel, and its outer skin, the work of Frédéric Bartholdi, who, some say, was thinking of his mother when he designed the lady's face (although he claimed he was after the "impassive" look of the Sphinx). After you pass the dark upward-sloping tunnel that leads to the torch (now closed, alas), the stairs get more cramped and steeper, until visitors are stacked in a sort of vertical-sardines effect. At the top you're rewarded with a view of the harbor and city through a row of brine-blurred windows. The biggest thrill? You got there! (P.S. If there should happen to be a thunderstorm, the interior lights will flicker wildly. Spooky!)

Incidentally, the small museum has an imposing copper replica of the statue's toe, a plaster model of the left ear, and a step-by-step explanation of how and why the whole magnificent creation was made and shipped. Make sure to find the small metal plaque on which Emma Lazarus's famous words "Bring me your tired..." are inscribed.

N.B. You can imagine what the Stature of Liberty gift shop has many images of. Enduring favorites are the foam crowns and the little statues made of something that looks like marble (also available on the ferry). The cafeteria will please you if you like fried food, and if you don't, try the acceptable sandwiches.

UrbanGlass

57 Rockwell Place, downtown Brooklyn
718-625-3685
www.urbanglass.com

Ages: 5 and up

**Getting there:
2, 3, 4, or 5 to
Nevins Street;
D, Q, R, or N
to DeKalb
Avenue**

Hard to categorize, memorable to visit, UrbanGlass is part workshop, part museum, and the largest art-glass-working center in the eastern United States. Located in a cavernous space right above an old theater in downtown Brooklyn, it has the feel of an inferno in a medieval painting: hot, *incredibly* hot, and dominated by three huge furnaces that glow with orange light.

Take advantage of a Sunday-afternoon open house (call for the schedule); they're free, and the kids will learn about glassblowing as it happens before their very eyes. The guided tours cover the gallery space and whatever exhibition is showing, but the highlight is to stand and watch as sweaty artists hoist globs of molten glass on long iron rods in and out of the "glory hole" (that's the furnace opening) and gradually shape them into objects of beauty. You also get to watch glass-bead making, hot glass casting (when glass is poured into a mold), and, if you're lucky, people working in neon. The environment feels risky, but it isn't, because everything is so carefully monitored. Still, you don't want the kids darting off here.

The special activity for the younger kids is sandblasting. You bring a glass bottle or mug (or buy one for $5), and the children decorate it with stickers and letters that are provided. Then the decorated items are put into a machine and literally bombarded with sand particles. When they emerge, they're frosted, except for the parts covered by the stickers. Peel off the stickers, and you have one cool souvenir! Children ages 12 and up can make an actual glass paperweight. Wearing protective goggles and standing right in front of the glory hole, they can work on the glass as far as their ability permits, closely supervised by their personal artist in attendance. Duration: 30 minutes; fee: $45, and you must book in advance. Note: This is a major treat for the right child.

The people involved in this enterprise are imaginative and enterprising. In the summer of 2000, they are holding the world's largest conference of glass artists (not open to the general public). To coincide with it, they're organizing the world's largest marble tournament, at Wollman Rink in nearby Prospect Park, along with an exhibit of historic glass marbles in the gallery inside the arch at

Grand Army Plaza. Check the Web site every so often to see what else UrbanGlass is up to. The small gift shop has many lovely pieces.

Washington's New York

Federal Hall National Memorial

26 Wall Street at Nassau Street
212-825-6888
www.nps.gov
Closed: Weekends

Ages: 5 and up

Getting there:
2, 3, 4, or 5 to
Wall Street; 1,
9, N, or R to
Rector Street

Fraunces Tavern Museum

54 Pearl Street at Broad Street
212-425-1778
www.nps.gov
Closed: Most major holidays
(except for July 4 and Washington's
Birthday)

Ages: 5 and up

Getting there:
4 or 5 to
Bowling
Green; 1 or 9
to South
Ferry; 2 or 3
to Wall Street;
N or R to
Whitehall
Street

Where Federal Hall National Memorial now stands, George Washington was sworn in as the nation's first president, in 1789. Six years earlier, in a second-floor room at an inn owned by a friend and fellow patriot, General Washington said farewell to the officers who had served under him in the Continental army. The two places offer complementary visions, public and private, of the father of our country.

Sitting at a confluence of small, antiquated streets, Federal Hall is dwarfed by the buildings surrounding it, but none have the majesty of this Greek Revival beauty, whose peaked roof conceals a Roman-style dome within. Children will be awed by the enormous statue of Washington on the steps; it looks so appropriate there that you'd think this must be the actual building where he took the oath. That building was, unfortunately, torn down in 1811.

The present building dates from 1834 to1842 and the exhibitions in the airy, echoey rotunda and galleries give its history by means of sweet intricate models, and a video that glides over the highlights in less than ten minutes. The most evocative object here is the Masonic Bible on which Washington actually took his oath of office (as did Harding, Eisenhower, Carter, and Bush). Be warned: It's a working Bible, and from time to time it's loaned out. Before you leave, go up to the mezzanine for a view of the rotunda.

Now head downtown, imagining the winding streets without skyscrapers, gridlock and vendors of dubious Rolexes. The task gets easier as the block on which Fraunces Tavern is located comes into view. The little group of five buildings is all that remains of the seventeenth- and eighteenth-century buildings here. The heavily restored tavern itself dates from 1719, and while the downstairs restaurant is called Fraunces Tavern and looks truly olde-Colonial, it has no connection with the original or with the museum.

The small permanent display is in the second-floor Long Room, where Washington met with his officers for the last time. The guests have just stepped out. Drinks have been poured, various board and card games are in progress, a cloak and a tricorn hat hang in the corner, clay pipes are everywhere and at a sideboard, someone's been decanting a bottle of wine. It's a hokey display, but it has real atmosphere, despite the emphatically plastic turkey on the buffet.

The third floor houses temporary exhibitions; it's worth going up just to ramble through two buildings' worth of oddly shaped rooms and sloping corridors with varying ceiling heights. They're the tipoff that these buildings are old.

The small gift shop has harmonicas, candy sticks in antiquated flavors (horehound, rum punch) and pretty, Shaker-style boxes. Buy the nifty postcard; it shows the museum block nestled in the shadows of the glass giants surrounding it.

N.B. If you visit during the summer months, you'll notice that this particular Nationally Registered Historic Place is well air-conditioned.

Weeksville Houses

**Old Hunterfly Road, 1698 Bergen Street bet. Buffalo and Rochester Avenues, Crown Heights, Brooklyn
718-756-5250
Open: Call for an appointment**

Ages: 6 and up

**Getting there:
3 or 4 to Utica Avenue**

Weeksville appears like a mirage: four modest wood-frame dwellings, sitting on an impeccable lawn in the shadow of the drab Kingsborough Houses. They are all that's left of a thriving free-black community of the nineteenth century, and they've seen a lot of history. It's their past thirty years that will appeal most to you and your children.

From the 1840s on, Weeksville was a tranquil, middle-class town, home to several distinguished black Brooklynites. As the demographics of the borough changed, it lost its specifically black identity and only a few locals remembered it. Then, in 1968, a professor and a pilot who were looking for traces of the old settlement flew over the area in a small plane and noticed the four little houses on a curving lane (Old Hunterfly Road) that bore no relation to the grid system. They'd found Weeksville just in time, because the rundown buildings were scheduled for demolition. Local schoolchildren, recognizing the site as an important part of their own heritage, started collecting money for its preservation. Grassroots action saved the Weeksville houses, and that's what keeps them open today.

Inside the houses you'll see period furnishings, and artifacts found at the site by archaeologists or donated by neighbors whose ancestors lived there. The old photographs are haunting, particularly a tintype of an anonymous young woman, in tight formal clothing, looking directly at the camera and thinking—who knows what? In order to see it all, you have to call and make an appointment, and then an interpreter will take you around, explaining not just what was found but how and the significance of this site to the community around it.

In short, this is an unusual museum. It's hard to see at the moment, but for a good reason. A desperately needed grant from the Borough of Brooklyn has made some restoration possible, and work will be continuing throughout 2000. When it's finished, the buildings will be thoroughly stable, Weeksville will be on the Internet, and a new building will contain an exhibition. During the restoration, the museum remains open, and you are welcome to see what's going on, so don't hesitate to call. And once you feel the history of this simple place, you'll probably want to make a donation yourself.

Whitney Museum of American Art

945 Madison Avenue bet. 75th and 76th St.
212-570-3600
www.whitneymuseum.com
Closed: Mondays

Ages: 6 and up

Getting there:
4, 5, or 6 to
72nd Street

As a parent, you'll immediately notice two things about the Whitney. First, this hulking granite building with its cool stone floors and high ceilings feels like a very good place to look at art. Second, the more you study the paintings and sculptures, the more you'll all have to talk about, since what's on exhibit is the social history of America as much as the art itself.

Among the sure kid winners here are the Georgia O'Keeffes, full of color and bold lines, the Joseph Stellas (compare his

Brooklyn Bridge with O'Keeffe's), George Bellows's looming and powerful depiction of Jack Dempsey in the ring, and Rockwell Kent's *The Trapper.* On a landing between the second and third floors, look for Charles Simonds's *Dwellings,* an eerie little model that looks like a ruined Pueblo village. (Look through the window on the landing below, and you'll see a sister-settlement on the window ledge of a building just across the street.) You'll love the

Edward Hoppers, but the children will be more interested in the Alexander Calders, particularly the renowned *Circus.* The de Koonings and Jackson Pollocks always make a strong impression; just remember to stress that some things should not be tried at home.

These are highlights in a large collection, not all of which can be shown at any given time. And since the museum is in the process of a major renovation, what's on show as of this writing will very likely change. Still, it's always worth a visit; there is so much here to provoke the kids' interest. Industrial landscapes and mountain ranges, people riding the subway or lounging at the beach, social protest and racial injustice, farmers and foundry workers, jazz musicians and nudes, the Stars and Stripes and soda-pop bottles: it all adds up to a portrait of the American experience that will seep into their minds, informing and enriching their sense of country.

These days, the Whitney cafe is run by Sarabeth's Kitchen; consequently, it's always crowded. There is, however, a small section to the side where you can help yourself to cookies, muffins, and sandwiches. At the gift shop, you'll find a small selection of cool, gimmicky, and pricey objects and T-shirts.

More Cultural Fun
for the Family...

Some museums that don't have permanent collections on show, or are not particularly kid-centric, nonetheless have some aspect that is wonderful for children. Among them are the following.

Cooper-Hewitt National Design Museum
(Smithsonian Institution)

2 East 91st Street, cor. Fifth Avenue
212-849-8400
www.si.edu/ndm
Closed: Mondays and federal holidays

Ages: 5 and up

Getting there:
6 to 86th or
96th Street

Great digs—the former mansion of Andrew Carnegie, no less—right in the thick of the big museum action (it's on Museum Mile). And it's the only museum in New York that's focused on design, which makes it immediately accessible to children. There are several family days through the year (from fall to spring), each one consisting of a guided tour of the current exhibition and an activity (if you were to guess "craft," you would probably be right). It's just a question of finding an exhibit that appeals to everyone—such as the recent, and wildly successful, "Unlimited by Design," where everything on display, from bathroom fixtures to pens to computer terminals, was designed to accommodate people of differing physical abilities and characteristics. The center-piece was a unique playground featuring many-tiered structures with ramps, steps, and some moving parts, all of it as safe and accessible as it was interesting and unusual.

Hudson Waterfront Museum

Garden Pier 45, 290 Conover Street,
Red Hook, Brooklyn
718-624-4719
Open: Only for special events

All ages

Getting there: A, C, or F to Jay Street/ Borough Hall, then B61 bus to Conover Street; For G to Smith-9th Streets, then B77 bus

Housed in an old barge that's moored in an atmospheric corner of Red Hook (cobblestones, pre-Civil War warehouses, sweeping views of the harbor), this little museum has assorted nautical items on display, but you can see them only during the summer, when David Sharps, waterfront connoisseur, juggler, and clown, opens up his wonderful space for some special programs for children. These dynamic and free-ranging events include "CIRCUSundays in June," and "Dancing in the Streets," dynamic, site-specific performances choreographed for Brooklyn children. "Dancing" usually happens in May, coinciding with the annual Brooklyn Waterfront Artists Coalition (BWAC) show, an arty extravaganza that's held in the gorgeous, high-ceilinged warehouses next door to the museum. There's food, live music, and the excitement of being on one of the last unspoiled stretches of

Brooklyn's old working waterfront. You'll feel the energy and creative flair of this doughty community as you breathe the sea air and stare at the Statue of Liberty, just across the water from the barge. So go. It's really worth the shlep. And you'll learn something about the history of New York's waterways, too. (Call to find out about the shuttle bus that runs from various points in Brooklyn to the barge.)

Pierpont Morgan Library

29 East 36th Street at Madison Avenue
212-685-0008
www.morganlibrary.org
Closed: Mondays

All ages

Getting there:
6 to 33rd
Street

Built specially to house its world-class collection of manuscripts, books, and prints, J. P. Morgan's stately library has many items that appeal to children, including Tenniel's illustrations for Alice's Adventures in Wonderland and glorious illuminated manuscripts. The problem is that only a fraction of the permanent collection is on show at any given time. Check listings of exhibitions and don't forget the two family days, one held in the spring and tied in to the current exhibition, the other at Christmas, when the original manuscript of *A Christmas Carol* is proudly displayed and the entertainment includes carolers, games, discovery hunts, magicians, and so on, as well as ceremonial readings from the book. The gift shop, incidentally, has exquisite children's books.

Museum of Chinese in the Americas

70 Mulberry Street at Bayard Street
212-619-4785

Ages: 6 and up

**Getting there:
6, J, M, N, R,
or Z to Canal
Street**

Too small for a special trip, the Museum of Chinese in the Americas is a poignant stop on a family visit to Chinatown. Go up a flight of wooden stairs in a big old schoolhouse, and you'll find this many-sided little place, shaped like a Chinese lantern. With a few objects and a lot of photographs and documents, it conjures up the hard world that Chinese immigrants faced when they came to America. Your children will immediately notice the colorful dragon and the phone box shaped like a pagoda; you can show them the heavy iron and laundry supplies and the tiny pair of embroidered shoes made for a woman with bound feet.

As the labels will tell you, the earliest Chinese immigrants left little behind them because their lives were so bare and framed by toil.

143

New-York Historical Society

2 West 77th Street at Central Park West
212-873-3400
www.nyhistory.org
Closed: Mondays, Tuesdays

Ages: Up to 6

Getting there:
1 or 9 to 79th
Street; B or C
to 81st Street

The prime attraction here: Kid City, an exhibition aimed at small children. A re-creation of a city block (Broadway between 82nd and 83rd streets) in 1901, it offers ample opportunity to build your own cityscape with blocks, dress up in period clothing and crash around with various household utensils and toys, or play at shopping in various re-created storefronts (featuring pretend food). There are ambitious concepts to tackle (comparing New York then and now), but your little ones will be content with the hands-on activities. Older children might enjoy a visit to the second-floor galleries, where Thomas Cole's heroic series of paintings, "The Course of Empire," is permanently on show. For one thing, the detail in Cole's pictures is great fun for kids—spot the lone hunter, the tiny eagle in the tree—and for another, Cole is dealing in mighty themes here in a wonderfully somber, Victorian way, tracing mankind's evolution and decay from the Savage State, through Consummation of Empire, all the way down to Desolation. The gift shop has excellent stuffed toys, tin toys, puzzles, and a fine range of Dover books.

North Wind Undersea Institute

610 City Island Avenue
(across City Island Bridge), Bronx
718-885-0701
Open: Call for schedule

Ages: 8 and up

Getting there:
6 to Pelham
Bay, then
BX29 bus

Closed for a major overhaul as of this writing, the North Wind Undersea Institute is an imaginative place housed in a picturesque Victorian mansion. Among the exhibits are anchors, cannon, all kinds of whaling tackle, nautical bits and pieces, and a life-size model of a sperm whale. But what you really go there for is a hands-on lesson in preserving marine life. To find out what precise form the workshops and tours will take, you'll have to call. Ask also whether it's possible to glimpse the seals who are trained to work for the police, retrieving sunken objects and rescuing humans from submerged vehicles. This is definitely worth a little research, since a City Island trip presents so many treats for the family, from the miniature golf course at Turtle Cove (at 1 City Island Road, 718-885-2646) to the fried-seafood joints at the water's edge.

P.S.1 Contemporary Art Center

**46-01 21st Street bet. Jackson
and Fourth Avenues,
Long Island City, Queens
718-784-2084**
www.ps1.org.
Closed: Mondays, Tuesdays

All ages

**Getting there:
E or F to 23rd
Street/Ely
Avenue; G to
Van Alst; 7 to
Courthouse
Square**

This big, red former public school just across the East River from Manhattan has for more than 20 years been at the heart of the New York art scene, and the exhibitions are full of the sort of modern art that kids love. We're talking multimedia, neon, video, performance art, and big, bold installations conveying enigmatic messages. Relax, and you'll love it too. There's outdoor music in the summer. And if you're in the mood, go to the Socrates Sculpture Garden and the Isamu Noguchi Garden Museum, both temptingly close by (see pages 120 and 108).

Queens County Farm Museum

**73-50 Little Neck Parkway nr.
Union Turnpike,
Floral Park, Queens
718-347-3276**
www.preserve.org/hht/hht.htm
Open: Daily (farmhouse only on weekends)

Ages: Up to 7

**Getting there:
E or F to
Union
Turnpike/Kew
Gardens, then
Q46 bus to
Little Neck
Parkway, walk
north three
blocks**

This working farm set on 47 acres offers a placid, bucolic experience, giving little city kids a taste of the farm life. The restored Dutch farmhouse (built in 1772) is not furnished, so the main attractions are the farmyard (with attendant animals), the fields (which museum staff and local volunteers plant with actual crops), the orchard and the hayrides. You can buy animal feed to hold under the nose of amenable baby goats or lambs; apart from that, you're not allowed to pet the creatures. For more excitement, visit during one of two special events. The Queens County Fair, held in September, is the real thing, with judging of prize animals, vegetables, and pies. Children can make apple cider and play assorted silly games, such as rubber-chicken throwing. The Thunderbird Native American Pow Wow, held every July in the apple orchard, is the region's largest pow wow, with serious dance competitions. Pow wows are a huge hit with most children, and understandably so. It's thrilling to watch the dancers wheel and stamp, their gorgeous costumes bedecked with feathers and quills. Stand by the drumming circle and watch how skillfully the chanting drummers pick up the rhythms from one another. The food is very kid-friendly (frybread, corn,) and so are the souvenirs (arrowheads, spears, and dream-catchers), so you'll probably end up spending more money than you expected to. By the way, next door is a private farm at which you can pay to have your children milk a cow, pick a pumpkin, or take a hayride. It may be a farm, but it's also a real New York operation and, despite the many smiling guides, doesn't feel very rural.

Some Great Museum Gift Shops: Beyond the Blue Hippo

Cool parents already know what a valuable resource they have in the city's museum gift shops. Whether it's tiny pewter knights in armor, activity kits, night-lights, scientific gizmos, or handsomely illustrated books, what's on offer beats the inventory of all but the most imaginative toy stores. Hands-down winners in this category are the lavishly stocked shops at the Metropolitan Museum of Art (which has, upstairs on the second floor, a children's gift shop full of games, toys, puzzles, inflatable mummies, castle kits, and books guaranteed to satisfy every Met-related need), the Museum of Modern Art, and the American Museum of Natural History (where the gift shops have just been revamped). In addition, we've select-ed a handful of other places that you should keep in your mind for occasions (birthday parties? Christmas morning?) when you might otherwise be stumped.

Alice Austen House Museum

Newly spruced up in a little room off the parlor, the shop has a wide range of old-fashioned toys at pocket-money prices. You'll get all teary at the sight of jacks for 92 cents (they're 10 bucks at the Guggenheim), small kaleidoscopes (the real ones, with glass bits inside) for $2, jump-ropes and Jacob's ladders, candy and whistles, paper dolls and teddy bears. And the adults can buy *Alice's World* ($22.50), an illustrated biography of the woman who lived here.

Brooklyn Museum of Art

There are two terrific gift shops here. The main shop has books and souvenirs related to its exhibitions, lovely objects and jewelry from around the world, and replicas of some of the museum's animal sculptures, which children will love. In the children's shop, called ArtSmart, you'll find all sorts of art, craft, and activity kits and supplies and other appealing and reasonably priced oddments: trouble dolls, Tutankhamen pencil cases and more.

Intrepid Sea-Air-Space Museum

This treasure trove of all things military and nautical is in the process of a renovation and expansion (including a new building). This means that, alongside the die-cast models of planes and boats, the Intrepid pens, caps, and keyrings and the NYPD-logo stuff, there's a full line of camouflage clothing (including spaghetti-strap tank tops for girls!). Other big sellers: the teddy bears (costumed as sailors and aviators) and 12" action dolls, for which you can buy 14 separate outfits. For those on a tight budget, the $2 sacks of 50 plastic soldiers or astronauts are a good buy.

Liberty Science Center

This huge gift shop stocks everything from freeze-dried ice cream and mod-els of body parts to vast arrays of Brio, Robotix and Puzz-3D and the New York City and Naval versions of Monopoly. There are seriously educational items—chemistry and meteorology sets, telescopes and microscopes—but also plenty of solar-system fridge magnets, "Roach Crossing" road signs, and, our favorite, models of the Hoberman Sphere in two sizes (neither of which, unfortunately, is electrically powered).

Lower East Side Tenement Museum

You'll all love this small but interesting gift shop. The mugs and T-shirts are tasteful, and there's a good selection of postcards and photographic books documenting the city's past. The chil-dren can pore over the well-selected period play-things, from little pop guns and cup-and-ball sets to chirping-bird tin toys, flip books, and finger puppets with wooden heads.

Museum of American Folk Art

Here, you'll find unusual items at all prices. We like the glycer-ine soap with a rubber duck inside, the Carmen Miranda paper doll, the revolving night-lights that project dreamy images onto the walls, the bike bells, the turtle flashlights and, at Christmastime, marvelous, soulful ornaments that you won't see anywhere else.

Museum of the City of New York

This inviting store is stuffed with New York City items: books, maps, posters, photographs. It has the requisite old-fashioned toys and nice MTA token and subway T-shirts (in black, which makes them cool). If you're feeling flush, ponder the wonderful skateboards with black-and-white cityscapes on them ($50).

National Museum of the American Indian

 The downstairs museum shop has plenty of evocative items at prices kids can afford: trouble dolls, arrowheads, ocarinas, woven yarn kick sacks, delicate little bark tepees, and stuffed critters of all sorts.

New York City Fire Museum

In addition to the authentic T-shirts, caps, and cloth or metal badges, you can buy rubber or plastic dalmatians in many sizes and  shapes, excellent pencils, puzzles and key rings, Curious George items, a nifty fireman transformer for $4, and (our recommendation) your very own small fireman for 75 cents.

New York Hall of Science

The gift shop here strikes a perfect balance between the seriously educational— binoculars, chemistry sets, fingerprint kit—and the endearingly goofy—lollipops with insects embedded, the redoubtable freeze-dried ice  cream, all manner of packaged slime. The price range is wide. And don't forget the penny-squashing machine in the dining area (see page 103).

Your Neighborhood Navigator

Brooklyn

Bronx

Queens

Long Island City

Staten Island

New Jersey

Index

About the Authors

Alfred Gingold and Helen Rogan have published numerous books and articles, including *The Cool Parents Guide to All of New York* and *Brooklyn's Best*. They live in Brooklyn with their son.

About the Illustrator

Catherine Lazure's drawings have appeared in the *New York Times* and many magazines, including *The New Yorker, Travel & Leisure, Town & Country, House & Garden,* and *Saveur.* She lives in New York City.

NEW YORK'S 50 BEST SERIES

GUIDES
TO THE
BEST OF
NEW YORK

New York's New & Avant-Garde Art Galleries $14.00

New York's 50 Best Art in Public Places $12.00

New York's 50 Best Places to Go Birding $15.00

New York's 50 Best Bookstores for Booklovers $12.00

New York's 50 Best Places to Have Brunch $12.00

New York's 50 Best Places to Discover and Enjoy in Central Park $12.00

New York's 50 Best Places to Take Children $12.00

New York's 50 Best Wonderful Little Hotels, 2nd edition $15.00

New York's 50 Best Places to Have a Kid's Party $12.00

New York's 100 Best Place to Have a Fabulous Party $14.00

New York's 50 Best Places to Find Peace & Quiet, 2nd edition $12.00

New York's 75 Best Hot Nightspots $12.00

New York's 100 Best Little Places to Shop $14.00

New York's 50 Best Skyscrapers $12.00

New York's 50 Best Places to Eat Southern $12.00

Brooklyn's Best: Happy Wandering in the Borough of Kings $14.00

Holiday Guide: Where to Eat, Shop and Celebrate $12.00

You can find these books at your local bookstore, through booksellers on the web, or by contacting City & Company directly.

Special editions can be created to specification.
Contact the Sales Director at:

City & Company   22 West 23rd Street   New York, NY 10010
tel: 212.366.1988   fax: 212.242.0415
e-mail: cityco@bway.net   www.cityandcompany.com